CAMBRIDGE LIBRARY COLLECTION

Books of enduring scholarly value

Printing and Publishing History

The interface between authors and their readers is a fascinating subject in its own right, revealing a great deal about social attitudes, technological progress, aesthetic values, fashionable interests, political positions, economic constraints, and individual personalities. This part of the Cambridge Library Collection reissues classic studies in the area of printing and publishing history that shed light on developments in typography and book design, printing and binding, the rise and fall of publishing houses and periodicals, and the roles of authors and illustrators. It documents the ebb and flow of the book trade supplying a wide range of customers with products from almanacs to novels, bibles to erotica, and poetry to statistics.

Roxburghe Revels, and Other Relative Papers

Lawyer, book collector and friend of Sir Walter Scott, James Maidment (1793–1879) displayed a talent for antiquarian research. Many of his works were printed privately in small quantities, such as the present publication, which first appeared in 1837. Established in 1812 and named after the great eighteenth-century book collector, the Roxburghe Club remains the oldest and most distinguished society of bibliophiles in the world. Joseph Haslewood (1769–1833), respected as an editor of early English literature, was a founder member and enjoyed the club's tradition of informal fun alongside more serious business. After his death, his manuscript account of these early activities, *Roxburghe Revels*, was unaccountably included in the sale of his books; extracts and critical comments on Haslewood and the club subsequently appeared in *The Athenaeum* in 1834. Maidment then prepared this defence, presenting and discussing his friend's remarks. The appendices include a biographical sketch of Haslewood.

T0371356

Cambridge University Press has long been a pioneer in the reissuing of out-of-print titles from its own backlist, producing digital reprints of books that are still sought after by scholars and students but could not be reprinted economically using traditional technology. The Cambridge Library Collection extends this activity to a wider range of books which are still of importance to researchers and professionals, either for the source material they contain, or as landmarks in the history of their academic discipline.

Drawing from the world-renowned collections in the Cambridge University Library and other partner libraries, and guided by the advice of experts in each subject area, Cambridge University Press is using state-of-the-art scanning machines in its own Printing House to capture the content of each book selected for inclusion. The files are processed to give a consistently clear, crisp image, and the books finished to the high quality standard for which the Press is recognised around the world. The latest print-on-demand technology ensures that the books will remain available indefinitely, and that orders for single or multiple copies can quickly be supplied.

The Cambridge Library Collection brings back to life books of enduring scholarly value (including out-of-copyright works originally issued by other publishers) across a wide range of disciplines in the humanities and social sciences and in science and technology.

Roxburghe Revels,

and Other Relative Papers

*Including Answers to the Attack on
the Memory of the Late Joseph Haslewood,
with Specimens of his Literary Productions*

EDITED BY JAMES MAIDMENT

CAMBRIDGE
UNIVERSITY PRESS

CAMBRIDGE
UNIVERSITY PRESS

University Printing House, Cambridge, CB2 8BS, United Kingdom

Published in the United States of America by Cambridge University Press, New York

Cambridge University Press is part of the University of Cambridge.
It furthers the University's mission by disseminating knowledge in the pursuit of
education, learning and research at the highest international levels of excellence.

www.cambridge.org
Information on this title: www.cambridge.org/9781108066907

© in this compilation Cambridge University Press 2014

This edition first published 1837
This digitally printed version 2014

ISBN 978-1-108-06690-7 Paperback

Painted by W. Hamilton R. A.   Engraved by E. C. Wagstaff.

JOHN KER, DUKE OF ROXBURGHE, K.G & K.T.

FISHER, SON & Cº LONDON, 1838

ROXBURGHE REVELS,

AND

OTHER RELATIVE PAPERS;

INCLUDING

ANSWERS TO THE ATTACK ON THE MEMORY OF THE LATE

JOSEPH HASLEWOOD, ESQ. F. S. A.

WITH

SPECIMENS OF HIS LITERARY PRODUCTIONS.

EDINBURGH:

PRINTED FOR PRIVATE CIRCULATION.

M.DCCC.XXXVII.

CONTENTS.

CONTENTS.

PREFATORY REMARKS.

Upon the demise of the late Mr. Joseph Haslewood, his library was brought to the hammer, and, amongst other curiosities exposed to sale, was a very remarkable MS. in which the acts and deeds of the Roxburghe Club were duly recorded. As those persons who were to be benefited by Mr. Haslewood's succession were not in such circumstances as to render a few pounds any object to them, it naturally excited considerable surprise, that this Volume, the contents of which were not calculated to reflect much credit on its author, should have been allowed to see light. It would appear, that of the two executors named in the will, one only accepted; and it is to be presumed, that this individual was not very well qualified to decide upon the literary merit of this production, otherwise it is hardly credible that he would have permitted its sale. Be this, however, as it may, the indefatigable Mr. Thomas

Thorpe bought the volume for forty pounds, and, subsequently, for a trifling advance, transferred it to the Editor of the
Athenæum, and the first use made of the purchase was a publication in the columns of that amusing journal, of the greater
part of its contents.

The extracts given were accompanied by observations, many
of which had better been spared, as they indicate by no means
an amiable spirit on the part of the commentator. Haslewood's birth, for instance, is made a matter of reproach,—his
personal deformity a subject of lampoon,—his harmless pursuits are ridiculed,—and he is throughout sneered at for his
desire to move in good society. All this is in the very worst
taste; the more especially as the gentleman attacked was a
person of an unoffending and amiable disposition. No doubt
his faults, as a writer, are many,—his style as vicious as can
well be conceived,—and his language far from grammatical;
still, notwithstanding these defects, he had his merits,—he
was eminently industrious, and particularly successful in gathering together curious facts which had escaped general notice.
In support of this assertion, we beg to refer to his notices of
the Old London Theatres, &c. which, as specimens of his merits
and demerits, have been included in the present volume.

Not content with bespattering the memory of poor Haslewood, the compiler of the Roxburghe Revels commenced an
attack upon the Club to which he belonged, and we cannot
refrain from briefly offering one or two observations on the
charges brought against it. In the outset, we may remark,
that we really are unable to see what right any one has to

find fault with a set of persons associating together for the sake of reprinting old books. If they choose to reprint "trash," let them do so,—it is their pleasure, and certainly no one else has any title to object. In the next place, the limitation of copies is objected to; but if the books are worthless, why should they be multiplied?

The fact is, that the books are *not* worthless, and, with very few exceptions, may be useful to persons attached to the Ancient History and Literature of their country. The object of the Club, and of all Clubs of a similar description, is not for *publication*, but *preservation*, and the object is fully attained by an impression of forty or fifty copies. If any one of the works is deemed interesting, there is no copyright to prevent a republication by booksellers; and, accordingly, it is admitted by the Editor of the Athenæum, that three of the Roxburghe publications have been republished in another shape. To multiply copies would serve no good end, for how few readers nowadays care one farthing about the works, however important, of the older authors! Even History, the study of which was once deemed useful, has been designated by an individual holding a high rank in the country, as merely ' An Old Almanack.'

Many years ago, the late Mr. Archibald Constable proposed to issue a series of reprints, a project which, under the Editorial care of the late Sir Walter Scott, he partially carried into effect. The works were intrinsically curious and valuable, and we justify this assertion, by stating, that Osborn's Traditionary Memoirs of James VI, Sir Philip Warwick's

Memoirs of Charles I, and the Autobiography of Lord Herbert of Cherbury, were amongst the number. Very few copies were sold, and the publisher was compelled to dispose of the remainder for little more than the price of waste-paper. More recently, the series of English Chronicles met with a similar fate; even English Poetry is at a discount, and accurate reprints of the works of many of our best ancient poets are seen tossing about the stalls for a shilling or two.

With the view of enabling such persons as were disposed to purchase the works originally issued by the Bannatyne Club, a certain number of copies were set aside, to be sold at very moderate prices. The importance of Spalding's Memoirs, and the Historie of King James the Sext, (a part of which was first published by Mr. Malcolm Laing) is pretty generally known to all students of Scotish History. These works were carefully edited, and, in every respect, well got up, but, nevertheless, the copies set apart for the public did not sell, and the result was, the Bannatyne Club declined, in future, printing any works for sale. In like manner, the Maitland Club printed some extra copies of a valuable Topographical History, but could get no purchasers. Of course, the attempt was not repeated.

The reason for all this is obvious,—there is no taste for books of this description, and a large impression would therefore tend to benefit only the printer and the papermaker. To expect Booksellers to risk such publications, is out of the question, and unless adopted by the Literary Clubs, it is extremely improbable that any valuable MS. would ever be printed.

In the present Miscellany, various amusing articles have been collected together relative to the Roxburghe Club, including the far-famed Revels,—portions of which might have been omitted, had this volume, of which only a few copies have been printed, not been intended for private circulation.*

* In the " Bibliotheca Selecta," as it is termed, recently published by Mr. Thorpe, a very singular Dramatic Collection by Mr. Haslewood (No. 656) occurs: It bears the following title, " Theatrical Manuscripts and Printed Collections relative to the English Stage; History of the Theatres and minor places of Public Amusements, compiled by the late Mr. Haslewood, in 9 volumes 4to, forming the most important and complete collection ever made upon the subject, and supplying unrivalled materials for publication, L.31. 10s." This is probably the article, page 76, and which was purchased for L.20.

The ensuing note in the Bibliotheca Selecta is curious:—" These collections, to the lover of the drama, will furnish an invaluable source of amusement, comprising an immense number of original extracts from early histories, poetical volumes, newspapers, periodicals, satires," &c. &c. the accumulations of a long life devoted to the pursuit, and frequently under circumstances highly favourable to the collector.

The Burney and other collections appear to have been most sedulously gone over, and the excerpts in manuscript, chronologically arranged. These form but a small portion, as there are many hundreds of advertisements from early newspapers and magazines."

Mr. Haslewood's announcement will best explain his original views in these collections.

" The following materials towards a HISTORY OF THE ENGLISH THEATRES IN LONDON, have been drawn from very promiscuous, very extensive, and very uncommon sources. Much from rare old publications, now little known, and still less attainable; a large proportion from public prints, things fallen into desuetude, and part from various MS. and other documentary evidence.

The origin of these volumes was a proposed attempt at a history of each play-house; the character it bore, openings and closings, uprising and downfalling in public favour, with public riots; a brief digression upon pieces that had a run, as, also, of proprietors.

I have not scrupled to embody much of the stage trickery: operas and concerts, of course, they are collaterals."

b

The Roxburghe Revels.

" Meanwhile my greatest source of comfort is the generous candour of Hazlewood."—
Guy Mannering.

" Perhaps it would be the best way to confide the whole secret to Hazlewood."—*Ibid*.

AMONG the late Mr. Joseph Haslewood's books was sold a MS., in his own hand-writing, to which he had given the following title :—' ROX-BURGHE REVELS; *or, an Account of the Annual Display, culinary and festivious, interspersed incidentally with Matters of Moment or Merri-ment. Also, Brief Notices of the Press Proceedings by a few Lions of Literature, combined as the Roxburghe Club, founded* 17th *June,* 1812.' The announcement of this work in the auctioneer's Catalogue ex-cited much astonishment. Mr. Haslewood, it was known, had not died in-solvent, or left a widow to struggle on with a large family ; he was a bache-lor of moderate fortune, who bequeathed his books and other property to

A

immediate, but not dependent relations, by whose direction, and for whose profit, this manuscript must have been offered *for sale!* On this strange proceeding we shall not stop to comment. It was enough for us to know that the work itself excited considerable interest, and we resolved therefore to purchase it at any price, that we might gratify curiosity, and give our readers its principal contents. We now set about the fulfilment of our design, in the course of which it will be necessary for us to speak pretty freely of the author, and to say something of most of the other " lions of literature combined as the Roxburghe Club." We hope and believe that we shall be able to execute our task without giving offence in any quarter. For any objectionable matter furnished by Mr. Haslewood, we cannot be answerable, and, most assuredly, upon nobody has he been so severe as upon himself. Before we have proceeded much farther, the reader will perceive in what way this " lion of literature" has been unsparing of his own reputation.

While living, Mr. Haslewood was a very cautious and politic man, and, had he extended this feeling to his death, few would have had reason to complain. Sprung from the very humblest class—we happen to know that he was born in Brownlow Street Lying-in Hospital—he never had any regular education, and he never remedied this original misfortune by subsequent exertion ; yet, by strange accidents, he was brought in contact with some of the most scholar-like, best informed, and most accomplished men of the age. Before these, he was generally reserved in conversation—careful to betray his ignorance as little as possible ; and, though he could scarcely open his mouth without committing an offence of some kind or other against his mother-tongue, he was prudent enough not to open it often in company where his blunders were likely to be detected. Where, however, he dare do so with impunity, he launched out with wonderful vivacity and assumption of importance ; and he persuaded some few, who were even less informed than himself, (they could not be many), to believe that he really was what he calls himself in conjunction with the rest of the Roxburghe Club, a " Lion of Literature." If he had termed himself " a lion of literature and alliteration," he would have been nearer the mark ; for his only *forte* seems to have been " affecting the letter." He had a sort of knack of this kind, and much of the rubbish he collected, and which was recently sold by Mr. Evans, was recommended to purchasers, about as sagacious as Haslewood himself, not by comical, but by coxcombical, titles.* In addition to these alliterative letterings, he " illustrated," as he termed it, his books by sundry manuscript notes, scarcely one of which did not betray the grossest ignorance, both of the subject and of the common grammatical modes of expressing an opinion. If Mr. Evans had selected only a few of these characteristic criticisms, they would have formed a most choice assortment of *Haslewoodiana*. The contrast between his caution when living, and his imprudence when dead, is remarkable. He was amazingly fond of fine words in his written compositions, and misapplied them in a manner never exceeded by the antiquated Mrs. Slipslop, or her modern imitator, Mrs. Malaprop ;—an important work was always " consequential," and an unimportant one " inconsequential ;"—a reference was generally " allusional," and sometimes " allusive ;"—a book seldom met with was " infrequential," and tracts corresponding in subject were " anomalous." When Mr. Haslewood edited any reprint, of which he did several, his unacknowledged obligations to the compositor, if not to the printer's devil, must have been very considerable.

The Roxburghe Club is now at an end : had its regular meetings been continued to the day of Mr. Haslewood's death, they could no longer have been held after the exposure he has made of the members and himself. How he contrived to become one of the number, is, to us, a mystery which possibly Dr. Dibdin could explain, for we do not think that at the sale of the

---

* Mr. Evans, who is an intelligent and judicious man, was almost ashamed of inserting them in his Catalogue, and never did so, without warranting himself, by informing the reader, that Mr. Haslewood had himself entitled such and such an assemblage of forgotten dulness— " Garlands of Gravity"—" Eleemosynary Emporium"—" Poverty's Pot Pourri"—" Wallat of Wit"—" Beggars' Balderdash"—" Octagonal Olio"—" Zany's Zodiac"—" Noddy's Nuncheon"—' Mumpers Medley"—" Quaffing Quavers to Quip Queristers"—" Tramper's Twattle, or Treasure and Tinsel from the Tewksbury Tank"—" Nutmegs for Nightingales" —all the merest nonsense in the world, the titles having little, and sometimes no relation to the contents of the volume.

library of the Duke of Roxburghe, in 1812, his purchases were sufficient in number or value to warrant his filling so prominent a station; and such men as the Duke of Devonshire, Lord Spencer, Lord Gower, Lord Morpeth, Sir F. Freeling, Mr. Baron Bolland, Mr. Justice Littledale, and others, must have felt themselves very ill-assorted, cheek-by-jowl, at a dinner-table at the Clarendon, with such a man as Mr. Haslewood, though a *soi-disant* " Lion of Literature." Attainments and talents level all ranks; but where were Mr. Haslewood's attainments?—where were his talents? and how will the well-educated and accomplished members of the Roxburghe Club get over the fact, that they, even once a year, associated with an individual who not only could contribute nothing to the stock of amusement (excepting, perhaps, as a butt,) but was in the habit of playing the spy upon their proceedings, and registering the follies, weaknesses, or unbendings,—call them what you will,—of the convivial board of the preceding day. *Dr. Dibdin seems to have been aware that such a record was kept,* for, on the 5th March 1827, the only occasion, we believe, when Haslewood was absent from the anniversary assembly, he tells him, in a note, that " his *chronicling* powers had been much needed," underscoring the word " chronicling"; and another member may have been also privy to it, as Mr. Haslewood records, that the particulars of what occurred had been furnished to him " by his accurate friend G. H. Freeling, Esq." However, we shall come to this date in the due course of the transactions, and it is time to insert Mr. Haslewood's account of the origin and formation of the Club. We must preface our first quotation, by observing, that the author seems to have taken especial pains with it, and that although it contains several inaccuracies and *Haslewood-isms*, we cannot help suspecting, that some other " Lion of Literature" had a finger in the correction of it. Here, again, possibly Dr. Dibdin could enlighten us.

" OF THE ORIGIN OF THE ROXBURGHE CLUB.

" The Roxburghe Club claims its foundation from the sale of the library of the late John Duke of Roxburghe, which commenced Monday the 18th day of May 1812, and extended to 41 days following, with a supplementary catalogue of three days, beginning Monday 13th July, with the exception of Sundays. The auctioneer was Robert H. Evans of Pall-Mall, being his first attempt to hold and heft the hammer, and the place of sale was at his Grace's late residence in St. James's Square.

"Upon Wednesday the 17th day of June, 'Il Decamerone di Boccaccio' was to be sold, and that lot being considered the rarest article in the whole of the Duke's library, (although no one then conjectured it would produce L.2,260,) the Rev. T. F. Dibdin, who therefore justly claims the title of Founder of the Club, suggested, some few days before the sale, the holding a convivial meeting at the St. Albans Tavern after the sale of that day. In consequence of that proposition originated the first of the following circular letters to those who assented to the meeting. The names of the gentlemen present on that occasion, and the resolution then adopted, was noted on the back of the letter of invitation immediately upon returning home. Similar memorandums were made in following years, and when omitted at the hour, were done so shortly afterwards, that it may be said the following papers contain an accurate history of the Club, which, to preserve, Charles Lewis, the binder of all the pieces distributed by the Club, gave same a clothing in April 1817."

We can only guess what Mr. Haslewood means by "heft the hammer," but Dr. Dibdin, in his "Biographical Decameron," (III. 51,) by a more figurative expression, explains it when he says, "Mr. Evans for the first time wielded the sceptre of dominion." How does the reader think he "wielded the sceptre of dominion?" Why, as the learned Doctor himself adds, "as a bookseller"! The figure is, therefore, at least appropriate.

We have never approved of the formation of the Roxburghe Club, or of the exclusive principle on which it was established; the realm of letters is, ought to be, and always will be, a republic—an oligarchy is not only odious, but impossible to be preserved. Neither are eating and drinking such intellectual occupations as well assort with the love of books; and when eating and drinking the *panem et aquam* degenerate into mere gormandizing and guzzling, as they did on every occasion when the Club met, whether annually or accidentally, we do not well see how the general cause of letters can be advanced by such proceedings.   The result, too, bears us out ; for in what department, let us ask, has this association been beneficial ? or how have the prints and reprints of neglected and deservedly-forgotten trash, made from time to time by the Club, been useful either to the living or the dead ?

The first specimen of authorship by the Club was not very favourable : it was in the form of a letter of invitation to certain noblemen and gentlemen to dine together—and how was it worded ?

" The honour of your company is requested to dine with the Roxburghe dinner on Wednesday the 17th instant."

We presume that this note was drawn up by Mr. Haslewood, who, as he could not be ornamental, tried to make himself useful ; and it is worthy of his pen : " to dine with the Roxburghe *diners*" might have been sense, or " to dine *at* the Roxburghe dinner " would have been better, but the Club, under the superintendence of the genius of Haslewood, scorned all common forms of expression, and therefore Lord Spencer was invited " to dine with a dinner."   What was the result?   The following met and dined on the 17th June 1812, at the St. Alban's Hotel :—

Lord Spencer, President—Lord Gower—Mr. Isted—Mr. Bolland—Mr. Laing—Mr. Freeling—Mr. Haslewood—Mr. Freeling, jun.—Mr. Heber— Sir Mark Sykes—Mr. Wilbraham—Mr. Dent—Mr. Phelps—Mr. Bentham —Sir Egerton Brydges—Mr. Utterson—Rev. T. C. Heber—Mr. Dibdin, Vice.

On the same occasion, a resolution was agreed to by the eighteen noblemen and gentlemen (" Lions of Literature ") present, that the Club should meet annually, and that it should be extended to twenty-four members : the following were therefore admitted *sur le champ* :—

The Duke of Devonshire—The Marquis of Blandford—Lord Morpeth— Mr. Ponton—Mr. Towneley—Mr Markland.

Mr. Haslewood is generally very particular, but he omits, on this occasion, to supply the important intelligence of the cost of the dinner to each individual—thereafter we shall find that he was minute, not only as to the price, but the bill of fare. On the next occasion, Lord Spencer was again in the chair, as President of the Club, and he was " faced," as usual, by Mr. (afterwards Dr.) Dibdin, and supported by all the members above enumerated, except the Duke of Devonshire, the Marquis of Blandford, (who, as the purchaser of the Valdarfer Boccacio, for L.2,260, ought, one would think, to have been present,) and Sir Mark Sykes. The proceedings we give in the words of Mr. Haslewood, whose clearness of style and accuracy of grammar are equally conspicuous.

" After Lord Spencer left the chair, who departed early, it was taken by Lord Gower, and the following resolutions were put and carried *nem. con.*

" That the Roxburghe Society should have an anniversary dinner on the 17th June, and the number of members be extended and limited to thirty-one.—That such meeting be held at the Saint Alban's Tavern.—That the mode of election, on any vacancy, should be by ballot, one black ball to exclude.—To fill up the vacancies beyond our original, of twenty-four, there *was* proposed, Lord Althorpe, elected unanimously, without show of hands —Rev. Rob. Holwell Carr—Mr. Joseph Littledale—Mr. Edward Littledale —Mr. Boswell—Rev. Mr. Dodd.

" Mr. Dibdin requested to take the office of Secretary [of course this could not be refused to him.]

" After Lord Gower left the chair, it was filled by Mr. Dent, and Dent and dullness are synonimous [we wonder Mr. Haslewood did not say " anonymous]." To him there succeeded Mr. Heber, with whom a select few tarried, that on arriving at home, the click of time bespoke a quarter to four.

" Dinner reckoning, L.50.

" Whip of half-crowns.

" Very inferior accommodation last year, but an excellent dinner this, moistened with champagne and claret.—*Da capo.*"

What Mr. Dent had done to excite Mr. Haslewood's spleen, that he should make his name synonymous with dullness, does not appear; but the chance is, that being a gentleman and a scholar, as well as a lover of old books, he felt, and possibly showed, his contempt for Mr. Haslewood: it could hardly be that he usurped a seat on this occasion which Mr. Haslewood thought

himself better qualified to have filled. It was at this meeting that a resolution was adopted for reprinting rare and curious pieces of " ancient lore,"
given by our author in the following form :—

" It was proposed and concluded for each member of the Club to reprint
a scarce piece of antient lore, to be given to the members, one copy being
on vellum, for the chairman, and only as many copies as members."

Here we see another objectionable point of exclusiveness, for if what was
reprinted were worth the trouble and expense, and would do any good to
the cause of letters, what an absurdity—a worse than absurdity—it was to
allow only one-and-thirty copies to be struck off. We are happy to say,
however, that the resolution of the Roxburghe Club has, at all events, done
little harm in this respect, for there are not perhaps four out of the forty-
four volumes, thus in the whole produced, that deserve reading, excepting
for some purpose purely antiquarian. Mr. Bolland (now Baron Bolland)
was the first to set the example, and we must do him the justice to say, that
his reprint of the ' Certaine Bokes of Virgil's Æneis,' translated by the celebrated Lord Surrey, is one of the few valuable contributions to the Society
and to society in general : hence they obtained admission into the collected
works of Surrey and Wyatt, by Dr. Knott. In the *Gentleman's Magazine*
for July 1813, may be seen a flaming account of the observance of the anniversary of that year, from the pen of Mr. Markland, under the signature of
Templareus. These " Lions of Literature," therefore, did not hesitate to
puff themselves into a little notoriety ; and here we are told that a seat at
the India Board, or a directorship of the Bank, were of less value, and would
be less eagerly sought, than a seat at the dinner table of the Roxburghe
Club !

It is to be observed, that in June 1813, the members were requested " to
dine with the gentlemen at Roxburghe Dinner ;" but, in the next year, Mr.
Haslewood's authorship for the card of invitation seems to have been again
in requisition, and Lord Spencer and the rest were called upon " to dine
with the Roxburghe Dinner." It would puzzle anybody but Beau Nash to
dine without a dinner, since the custom of dining with Duke Humphrey
went out of use. On this occasion, twenty-one out of the thirty-one sat

down to table, and their proceedings are thus recorded by the pen of the immortal author of the " Roxburghe Revels."

" A motion was made, but negatived most properly, for an encrease of members.

" After Lord Spencer left the Chair, it was taken, I believe, by Mr. Heber, who kept it up to a late hour : Mr. Dodd very volatile and somewhat singular, at the same time quite novel in amusing the company with Robin Hood ditties and similar productions. I give this on after report, having left the room very early from severe attack of sickness which appeared to originate in some vile compound partook of at dinner :

" The charge was L.2, 5s. p. man, and the wine alleged to have been drank in a proportion of excess that must have intoxicated every one. It was generally believed that the next dinner wo^d not be had at the same place.

" N. B. Mr. Bolland's reprint was not ready."

The Rev. Mr. Dodd, here celebrated, was one of the Masters of Westminster School—a man whom we have good reason to remember—a great collector of old plays and poetry, and especially mad on the subject of ballads relating to Robin Hood and his fellow outlaws. He died in 1818, but until that year, the Roxburghe Club was annually enlivened by his chants, which sometimes held the company over-long, as we used to hear sundry members complain. On the 17th of June 1814, poor Mr. Haslewood seems early in the evening to have been assailed by a " severe attack of sickness," which he attributes to some " vile compound *partook* of at dinner ;" we apprehend that it proceeded from some vile compounds partaken of after dinner ; but, whether one or the other, he certainly was not in a condition to know whether Mr. Heber did or did not take the chair after Lord Spencer left it. We conclude, that his Lordship abandoned the room about the time when Mr. Haslewood began to be afflicted.

Mr. Richold, of the St. Alban's Tavern, got into sad disgrace, for his real or supposed overcharge for wine on this occasion ; but had all the members been as much *overcharged* as Mr. Haslewood confesses himself to have been, perhaps, after all, there was no great reason to complain of the bill, and of the " L.2, 5s. p. man." The next field-day was held at Grillion's Hotel, and here, the worthy proprietor, obviously having no respect for Mr. Haslewood's powers of composition, wrote the invitation himself, and nothing, therefore, could be more properly worded. Twenty members assembled under the chairmanship of Sir Mark Masterman Sykes, for nobility and its scions this day were absent. The persevering non-attendance of one or more of the most distinguished members, led to the adoption of a resolution, that any one who was absent for five successive anniversaries, should be considered as no longer belonging to the association. On this occasion it was, that Mr. Bolland's reprint of " Lord Surrey's Translation of part of the Æneid," was distributed among the members ; and it was agreed, that the order of the alphabet should be pursued, as regarded these donations, for the future ; but our annalist adds, with his usual choice phraseology, that it was agreed, that any member might go out of this course if he thought fit.

The bill on this occasion amounted to L.57, or L2. 17s. p. man, and in this instance we are furnished with all the interesting minutiæ of the dinner, and the number of bottles of each sort of wine, according to which, these twenty " Lions of Literature," managed to dispose of drinkables to the extent of about L.33, at one sitting.*

---

* The authorship of Grillion's French waiter is to the full as well worth preserving as that of Mr. Haslewood ; and we, therefore, give the " reckoning" with " all its imperfections on its head."

" Dinner du 17 Juin 1815

20	20	0	0
Desser	2	0	0
Deu sorte du Glasse	1	4	0
Glasse pour 6	0	4	0
5 Boutelle de Champagne	4	0	0
7 Boutelle de harmetage	5	5	0

Then we come to an interesting and highly characteristic anecdote, which we give in the very words of our author :—

" June 27, 1815.

" At the meeting upon the 17th a question was agitated between Sir Mark M. Sykes and Mr. Dent as to whether that was the third or fourth anniversary meeting, which originated in a miscalculation by reckoning the first dinner an anniversary one.   The common result among Englishmen followed : i. e. a wager, the stakes being the celebrated —— against the renowned Livy.   However the subject becoming general conversation and the magnitude of the articles pitted, somewhat considered, Mr. Heber very adroitly turned what must have proved dissatisfaction to one member and not a very covetable triumph, as between gentlemen, to another, into a general booze, by remarking, in a neat speech, that each party must be loth to part with so choice a specimen, and suggested varying the wager into a dinner for the company.   That was properly acceded to by the contending parties, and this was settled as a festivous day extraordinary.   Upon the point in

1 Boutelle de Hok	0	15	0
4 Boutelle de Port	1	6	0
4 Boutelle de Maderre	2	0	0
22 Boutelle de Bordeaux	15	8	0
2 Boutelle de Bourgogne	1	12	0
(Not legible)	0	14	0
Soder	0	2	0
Biere e Ail	0	6	0
Por la Lettre	0	2	0
Pour faire un prune	0	6	0
Pour un fiacre	0	2	0
	55	6	0
Waiters	1	14	0
	57	0	0

dispute being decided, Mr. Heber further remarked that after the specimen of reprint just distributed it would add zest to the proposed meeting if some gentleman would volunteer a copy of a work upon that occasion : whereupon the writer (but, whether *adroitly* or not, let others report), submitted to the Chairman, that from no other member could such an article be with more confidence expected than from Mr. Heber, as his store was too great for any difficulty to exist beyond selection.   The reply complimentary was, perhaps, too hastily uttered, as Mr. Heber observed he only needed the editorial industry of the writer to assist him in completing such an undertaking.   Hereupon the retort, prompt, signified if only editorship was required, such assistance, if Mr. Heber thought it worth requesting was at his service, nor should the Club ever lose such an advantage by the need of that labour.   This was handsomely accepted.   Let it not pass unobserved this was on Saturday the 17th, and on the tenth day therefrom the volume must be ready to distribute.   However short the space, unheeded went the 18th, and unheeded went the 19th, but in the morning of the 20th a verbal message requested Mr. Heber might be met at Evan's Sale Room, Pall Mall, at 4 o'clock.   Here the first natural enquiry was if out of the influence of cups the confidence remained for accomplishing the proposed reprint.   A reply given in the affirmative produced the work."

The work was T. Cutwode's *Caltha Poetarum ; or, the Bumble Bee,* a rare collection of almost worthless poetry, then supposed to be *unique,* but now known to be otherwise, as a perfect copy of the book was sold by auction by Sotheby, a week or two ago, to Mr. Freeling, for L.8, 5s. The above particulars are followed by Mr. Haslewood, with some tedious and silly details, regarding the eight days occupied in printing and getting up this production, which did not contain nearly so much letter-press as a single side of a newspaper, of which four sides are composed and published every day : yet our author talks of it as a most astonishing achievement, and of himself as the great achiever in the capacity of Editor, whose duty was merely to see that the reprint corresponded with the original.

The following is part of what Mr. Haslewood inserts upon the subject —

" June 20th, Obtained the Poem.—21st, Transcribed.—22nd, Printed.—23rd, Revised and pulled off.—24th, Hot-pressed.—25th, Dies non —26th, Bound.—27th, Distributed.

" The Bumble Bee of the title was cut in fac-simile. In the first title was introduced a marygold, and upon my suggestion printed in natural colours. It is proper to observe here that only by the ready assistance and extreme exertion of Mr. Bensley's people could this have been accomplished. Some marks of this rapid progress may be traced in some inconsequential variations which could not easily be avoided under such circumstances. The only absentees from the dinner of those present upon the 17th were Mr. Jos. Littledale from indispensible business, and Mr. Utterson from expecting the needless etiquette of a further invitation."

The wager-dinner, that highly intellectual treat, to settle a dispute of so much importance, between two redoubtable " Lions of Literature," took place on the 27th of June.

The anniversary of the 17th of June 1816, was celebrated with more than usual splendour : twenty-three members put their feet under Grillion's mahogany, and the Duke of Devonshire was for the first time of the party. Lord Spencer was in the chair, and he was supported, besides the Duke, by Lords Gower, Morpeth, and Althorp, and the usual attendants.

" At this meeting (says Mr. Haslewood, though, like Pope ! he may be ' known by his style') the reprints were no less than four in number—viz.

" Lord Spencer the first three books of Ovid by Thom^{s}. Churchyard 1578. —Mr. Boswell Poems of Richard Barnfield 1598 —Mr. Freeling Dolarnys Primrose 1606.—Mr. H. Freeling Newes from Scotland 1591.

" This latter gentleman diversified the plan by the novelty of distributing under each plate at dinner, a copy of a French poem printed b. l. and entitled *La contenance de la Table*. It was of a size different from any that had before appeared, being of a kind of square 12mo, or like old fashioned Tables of Interest; and in troth had much interest therein, but it may be right here to record the general size of the club book which is small or pot quarto.

" Promises for the next year were very numerous : to name and the announcement to be forgotten, may turn this suppositively into an invidious chronicle.

" Hilarity and cheerfulness turned out the night and wore upon the morning, the star of which seemed rather to lack some of its wonted brilliancy, however there was proof of the magnet not having lost any of its powers as several of the members who had hitherto stole away shortly after the hour of ' go to bed Tom' were found loitering even after the single stroke had ceased sounding of the ' mighty Tom.' "

All this is very curious and edifying, from the " *pot* quarto" size of the reprints, than which nothing could be more appropriate, down to the " mighty Tom" hour to which the soakers sat.   On this occasion they consumed eatables and drinkables to the tune of L.62, 13s. 6d.   " Lions of Literature," indeed ! It would have been worth something to have seen these lions at feeding time.   As Mr. Cross's man used to tell the visitors at Exeter Change, " Sir they eats with a woraciousness that is wery extonishing"—a sentence worthy of the great Haslewood himself.

The Club did not assemble the next year at Grillion's, but at Jacquiere's, the Clarendon.   Probably, economy was the main object, for the dinner and wine for twenty-two members only cost L.49.   Among the names, occurs that of Mr. Hibbert for the first time, who had been elected in the preceding year to fill the vacancy occasioned by the first death in the Club, that of the Rev. T. C. Heber.   " Our dinner (observes our gifted author) was tolerable, and the wines tolerable, but neither Richold, Grillion, or Jacquiere, condescended to consider us as superlatives, and tolerable treatment is not sufficient."   The waiters had, perhaps, reported to their masters some of the conversation in which Mr. Haslewood took part : hence, the little respect with which they were treated.   " We have been forced (adds our author, with a brilliant refinement of humour) to copy the comet in our wandering, and it is doubtful if we are yet become fixed stars."   Imagine a comet stumping from hotel to hotel with a club-foot.

Seven reprints were distributed among the members, but the only one of any value was the interlude of 'The World and the Child,' presented by Lord Althorp, which, notwithstanding the exclusive and cautious spirit of the Roxburghe Club, has found a place in the 12th volume of the last edition of Dodsley's Old Plays. Mr. Haslewood thus enumerates the book benefactions :—

" A proper new Interlude of the World and the Child, otherwise called mundus et infans ; L. Althorp.—The Glutton's Fever by Thomas Bancroft ; Mr. Phelps.—Cock Lorell's Boat. A Fragment—Rev. Henry Drury.— The Funerals of K. Edw. the Sixt ; Mr. Dodd.—Hagthorpe Revived or Specimens of a forgotten Poet ; Sir S. E. Brydges.—Le Liore du Faulcon ; Mr. Lang.—Istoria novellamente ritrovata di duo nobile amanti, &c. : William Holwell Carr. Of these presentments perhaps the most rare and curious was that of L^d. Althorp. Only a single copy of the original edition is known, and that belongs to the library of Trinity College, Dublin. The history of its coming to this country is of a felonious nature, and may be recounted at some future period."

The " history of its coming to this country," regarding which such a fuss is here made, is merely this—that the interlude of ' The World and the Child,' was stolen from Trinity College Library, Dublin, sold to a London house, and, being innocently bought by them, was as innocently resold to the agent of Lord Spencer, by whom, on an explanation of the fact, it was, of course, immediately relinquished.

The next anniversary was celebrated at the Albion, in Aldersgate Street, and not a single nobleman could travel so far east as to be present at it— Mr. Heber was in the chair, and the Rev. Mr. Carr, Vice, *vice* Dr. Dibdin. The list of the company is given by Mr. Haslewood, followed by such excuses as he could find for absentees, and an account of the donations in the shape of reprints, &c.

" Our meeting this year was remarkable in respect of more presentations than either of the preceding anniversaries, and yet, at the same time, the company fewer in number than any preceding day. Our number at dinner was only 15 to assign an apology for absentees may be easily done and therefore no foundation exists to fancy there was a falling off of the Club. The recent death of Lady Althorp occasioned the absence of our usual Chairman and of course his son. The Duke of Devonshire and Mr. Dibdin were abroad. The general election made absentees of Ld Morpeth, Sir M. Sykes, Sir E. Brydges, Mr. Dent, and Mr. Bolland. Rev. Hen. Drury from the accident of breaking his arm: Henry Freeling in Cornwall for benefit of his health and E. V. Utterson at —— because his wife was there.

" But the nine copies.

" The Life of St Vrsula, and Guiscard and Sigismund; the Duke of Devonshire.—Balades and other Poems by John Gower; Earl Gower.—The Complaint of a Lover's Life, and, controversy between a Lover and a Jay; The Rev. T. F. Dibdin.—Chester Mysteries. De Beluvio Noe. De Occisione Innocentium; Mr. Markland.—The Chorle and the Bird; Sir M. M. Sykes.—Diaphantus or the Passions of Love; Mr. Wilbraham.—Diana, or the excellent conceitful Sonnets of H. C.; Mr. E. Littledale.—Ceremonial of the Marriage of Mary Queen of Scots, &c.; Mr. Bentham.—The Solemnities and Triumphes doon and made at the Spousells and Marriage of the Kings Dorghter &c.; Mr. Dent."

Nevertheless, although only fifteen sat down, they seem to have eaten and drank for the whole club; it was, as Wordsworth says, " forty feeding like one," and the bill at the conclusion of the night amounted to—how much does the reader imagine?—L.85, 9s. 6d.—for feasting fifteen " lions," or L.5, 14s. per beast ! *—" Your cits (says Mr. Haslewood, with true west-end-of-the-town vulgar complacency and affectation) are the only men for a feast; and, therefore, behold us like locusts, travelling to devour the good

---

* The bill, as a specimen of the advantages of separate charges, as well as on other accounts, may be worth preserving in a Note:—

ALBION HOUSE.

June 17, 1818.

Bread and Beer...	0	9	0
Dinners.....................................	9	9	0
Cheas and Butter..	0	9	0

things of the land, eastward, ho! At a little after seven, with our fancies
much delighted with inspecting the first eight in the above list (the last not
being then delivered) and according to the rump-placement [elegant and refined waggery!—what a treat must his conversation have been!] already

Lemons	0	3	0
Strong Beer	0	9	0
Madeira	3	3	0
Champagne	2	11	0
Saturne [sic in MS.]	1	4	0
Old Hoc.	4	16	0
Burgundy	0	18	0
Hermitage	0	18	0
Silery Champagne	0	16	0
Sherry	0	7	0
St. Percy	2	11	0
Old Port	2	9	0
Claret	11	4	0
Turtle Punch	0	15	0
Waxlights	2	10	0
Desert	6	6	0
Pine-ice creams	1	16	0
Tea and Coffee	1	8	0
Liqueures	0	14	0
2 Haunches of Venison	10	10	0
Sweet sauce and dressing	1	4	0
50 lbs. Turtle	12	10	0
Dressing do	2	2	0
Ice for Wine	0	6	0
Rose Water	0	5	0
Soda Water	0	12	0
Lemons and Sugar for do	0	3	0
Broken Glass	0	5	6
Servants dinners	0	7	0
Waiters	1	0	0
	85	9	6

given, we fifteen sat down." The bill of fare seems to have been as follows, and we have appended to it some of our author's sagacious and sportive remarks :—

First Course.

Turtle.*

Turtle Cutlets.   Turtle Fin.

Turbot.

Boiled Chickens.   Ham.

Soutee of Haddock   Chartreuse.

Turtle.   Frame.   Turtle.

Tendrons of Lamb.   Fillets of Whitings.

Tongue.   John Dory.   R. Chickens.

Turtle Fin.   Fricandeau of Turtle.

Turtle.*

†‡† Cold Roast Beef on Side Table.

* These Tureens were removed for two dishes of White Bait.

Second Course.

Venison (2 haunches.)

Third Course.

Larded Poults.

Tart.   Cheese Cakes.

Artichoke bottoms.

Jelly.   Prawns.

R. Quails.   R. Leveret.

Salade Italien.   Creme Italien.

Peas.

Cabinet Pudding.   Tourt.

R. Goose.

" Consider in the bird's eye view of the banquet, the trencher cuts, foh! nankeen displays : as intersticed with many a brilliant drop to friendly beck and clubbish hail, to moisten the viands, or cool the incipiant cayenne. No unfamished liveryman would desire better dishes, or hightasted courtier better wines. With men that meet to commune, that can converse, and each willing to give and receive information, more could not be wanting to promote well-tempered conviviality ; a social compound of mirth, wit, and wisdom. Combining all that Anacreon was famed for, tempered with the reason of Demosthenes and intersected with the archness of Scaliger. It is true we had not any Greek verses in praise of the grape, but we had as a tolerable substitute the ballad of the Bishop of Hereford and Robin Hood sung by Mr. Dodd : and it was of his own composing. It is true we had not any long oration denouncing the absentees, the cabinet counsel, or any other set of men, but there was not a man present that at one hour and seventeen minutes after the cloth was removed but could not have made a Demosthenic speech far superior to any record of antiquity. It is true no trait of wit is going to be here preserved for the flashes were too general, and what is the critical sagacity of Scaliger compared to our Chairman. Ancients believe it we were not dead drunk and therefore lie quiet under the table for once and let a few moderns be uppermost."

Such was Mr. Haslewood's notion of the vivacious : the flashes of wit among the company were, however, " too general" to be preserved, but the diners at L.5, 14s. per head were all men who " met to commune, and could converse," and there was not one present " who could not have made a Demosthenic speech far superior to any record of antiquity." We would have given as much money as each paid only to hear Mr. Haslewood make the attempt. His " reason of Demosthenes," and " archness of Scaliger," are fine touches of critical discrimination. But, great as were his powers of wit and eloquence, if the reader will cast a look upon the following, he will see that Mr. Haslewood had still an eye to the main chance, and he thus acutely reasons upon the expense of the dinner :—

" According to the long established principles of " Maysterre Cockerre" each person had L.5, 14s. to pay, a tremendous sum, and much may be said

thereon.—Economy—To print jointly—Charity—Engrave the Chairman—
and other heads as numerous as the words in Cooper's Lexicon, might be
propounded by the voice of costive frugality : but why need we care all our
banquets will be paid for roundly to our executors, always provided we die
before we are beggars and have assignees. Let us canvass this methodically.
—Lay down a principle that the logic of Oxford and mathematics of Cambridge cannot overturn. Thus it is. A certain bookseller, (and booksellers
we know are the most uncertain in their dealings of any race of tradesmen,
but this particular one, was an *arch* one, and therefore a certain bookseller)
observed he would venture to give L.15 per copy for a complete set and that
his brother he thought would go even to L.20, if a complete set co^d be obtained. Now for a complete set of the club tracts to be sold a member must
go off insolvently, if not hastily, and then the inference is some half a dozen
dinners which cost between L.20 and L.30 obtains 21 books and take each
copy at an average value, far under the opinion of those arch estimators,
because we will only pay L.10 p. piece or L.210 for the whole a balance remains between L.180 or L.190 go to, the price weighs not. And if it did,
think of the great value of notoriety."

To this succeeds a capital puff—*i. e.* a puff in capitals, transmitted by
the body for insertion in the *Literary Gazette,* and a farther notice, of which
the Rev. Mr. Carr, vice-president for the day, was the author, inserted at his
request in the *New Times.* An account of the celebration of the Roxburghe
anniversary, at Paris, where Dr. Dibdin was temporarily residing, appeared
in the *Morning Chronicle,* at the instance of Mr. Haslewood. The members
were, therefore, fully sensible of the " great value of notoriety," and these,
we suppose, were among the *press proceedings,* noticed so emphatically by
the author in his title-page to the book before us.

The chaunter of Robin Hood-ballads, the Rev. Mr. Dodd, died on August
27, 1818, and it became a question who was to occupy his chair at the dinner-table. A hint was given by Mr. Haslewood to Mr. Bliss, the son of a
bookseller at Oxford, that he might put in his claim to fill the vacancy in
the club. Mr. Bliss, however, seems, from his letter, to have modestly
thought that he could have no chance in the competition, " though (he ob-

serves) there are few things that would have given me more satisfaction
than to have joined a society so congenial to my own taste and pursuits."
We suppose that he alludes to the eating and drinking propensities of the
body ; or, he may possibly refer to the book-making sort of appendix to
their festivities. Nobody seems to have dreamt of Mr. Bliss but his friend
Mr. Haslewood, who himself says, that when Mr. A. (afterwards Sir Alexander) Boswell was proposed to the club on the 19th of February, 1819,
there was not a moment's hesitation nor a dissentient voice. A dinner was
consumed on the event, for nothing could be done without " another gorge,
and then another :" it was given at the Clarendon, to which the vagrant
Roxburghers had returned. This, it will be remarked, was an extra feed,
and only cost L.39 for fifteen eaters and drinkers.

On the morning of June 17, 1819, an important event occurred. The
Valdarfer Boccacio, which had been bought by the Marquis of Blandford
(now become Duke of Marlborough) for L.2,260, and in which the Roxburghe Club originated, was resold at Evans's rooms, in Pall Mall, for only
875 guineas. It had been seized with the rest of the White-Knight's
library, and was brought to the hammer to satisfy creditors. His Grace
could not, however, bear the notion of parting with it, and, on the morning
of the sale, wrote the following note, marked " Immediate," to Triphook,
the bookseller :—

" TRIPHOOK,—I beg you will purchase the Valdarfer Boccacio for me,
for anything *not exceeding* L.1500 : and, should the deposit-money be necessary, I will give it you, if you will call *tomorrow* or *Saturday.*

" Your's &c.,
" MARLBOROUGH."

" Holles-st. Thursday,
    June 17. 1819."

Now, Triphook was a cunning, though not always a prudent, man, and
he shrewdly guessed that, as the Duke's books were sold to pay some of his
debts, his Grace would not be able to produce the purchase-money, or even
the deposit, either " tomorrow," " Saturday," or any other day. Accordingly, he refrained from executing the commission, and Mr. Haslewood tells

us, that " the Decameron was knocked down to Griffiths, the deputed agent, to make a petty, meddling-speculation for the all-grasping house of Longman & Company, who, as soon as they possessed the volume, began to be nervous, fevered, and bewildered with the dread of continued possession, and they besought Earl Spencer to take it off their hands at the 875 guineas. There was not the smallest pecuniary or other advantage made by the purchase, if we except the useless puff [how a *useless puff* could be an exception we are not informed] THE GREAT HOUSE BOUGHT THE BOCCACIO !—Have done with the petty fry Longman, Hurst, Rees, Orme, &c."

Earl Spencer presided at the dinner which followed the sale of the Valdarfer Boccacio : twenty-one members sat down to table, at Jaquiere's, and the bill was comparatively moderate, L.55, 13s. Mr. Haslewood says, with characteristic sprightliness, " Twenty-one members met joyfully, dined comfortably, challenged eagerly, tippled prettily, divided regretfully, and paid the bill most cheerfully." We conclude, that Jaquiere, by this time had taken the hint, and treated Mr. Haslewood and the rest as "superlatives." It was on this occasion that the Club adopted the resolution to erect a tablet to the memory of Caxton, in Westminster Abbey, or St. Margaret's.

By the 17th of June in the next year, the tablet, which was designed and executed by Westmacott, was finished; but it is here necessary to quote our author, who inserts the following paragraph, under the head of " Anniversary 1820."

" Jacquiere *carded* us in usual manner, nor are there any tricks in his cards that a man who has a queasy stomach towards gaming, may not swallow. Dinner was to be at 7 precisely, and as an auxiliary summons a letter from the V. P.—which peruse. The " especial business" that needed the clustering in conference before the summons of grace, was neither more or less, than to get rid of an unworthy member : attempted indirectly more than once before, and little question of a majority at any time. Still we are gentlemen, and it is at last but vulgar, where absence, as a member, is the legible height and front of his offence—to expel. And this inference must serve as an apology that the D. of M. has yet a right to bum-chair among us, tho' he has never condescended to do it."

After giving the names of those who sat down " yfere," Mr. Haslewood jocosely adds, " It likes me well—a goodly set—twenty-five out of one-and-thirty, let me tell you, [posterity we presume] is a spanking majority."   It was on this day that our author contributed his reprints of ' Jack Juggler' and ' Thersites,' to the stock of the Club.   How competent he was to the task of editing such pieces, may be judged from the pitiable blunder he made when speaking of these two ancient dramas in the British Biographer: where he said, that they " took precedence of the earliest specimen yet known of an interlude unconnected with scriptural history."   He knew nothing of all the moralities written from the reign of Edward IV. downwards, or he could never have committed so gross an error.   Such is the result when such men are allowed to put pen to paper.   Their friends ought to take better care of them.

The cost of the dinner to five-and-twenty was not so outrageous as usual, only L.65, 12s. 6d., and Mr. Haslewood, for the first time, takes some credit to the Club for abstemiousness.   " There is a beauty, however mediocre, in banquetting rationally," he observes, and then congratulates himself, that the lessons of the old school are now nearly obsolete," following it up by the subsequent passage, the full meaning of which we do not profess to have discovered :—

" It is no longer requisite to gobble solids and drench fluids until every two out of three of the company appear stupid with gormondizing, or asleep with intoxication : that is where the set too proves (what it seldom does with pulings) so innoxious as not to force accounts to be cast up before the bill arrives.   Nor does the new plan, a voluntary pressure of the vintage cup, prevent the appetite being satiated.   The ancient return of ' Dead and alive,' of ' stickers and stayers,' of ' cutters and runners' may even now be made at midnight to wives (dearly loving) and lesson giving matrons, hight mothers, (of unceasing affection) if needful.   The difference is he, now disguised, puts on his mask and mantle by choice, formerly he was overpowered by an attentive chairman with noisy caution denouncing sky-lights and heel-taps.   And yet we find men tippy, for there is such a thing still as seduction, although involuntary.   Good conversation and good wine forms a social compact, and to find in such cases Roxburghers have taken what is fancied as too much, when they scarcely believe, half enough is taken, from the enjoyment, seems pardonable."

Two resolutions seem to have been adopted at this meeting—that three consecutive absences should be considered a secession from the Club, (by which, Mr. Haslewood states, " more was meant than meets the eye,") and that two guineas be contributed towards the monument to Caxton. We hope, for the credit of the rest of the Club, that the bad English of the following note, appended to the resolutions, is to be attributed to the writer of the ' Roxburghe Revels.' " The monument is now finished, and is ready *to fix* up." Mr. Haslewood was not bound, nor, indeed, expected, to know the difference between verbs active or passive, neuter or transitive, only care should have been taken by the Club to correct his mistakes ; but their business as " Lions of Literature" was to eat and drink, and that they did to perfection.

All that was worth notice in the proceedings at the next anniversary (if anniversary that may be called, which was held on the 18th of June, the day after the usual period,) was communicated by Mr. Haslewood, and some of the other notoriety-loving members to the *Gentleman's Magazine*. The cost of the entertainment was L.55, 11s. 6d. for twenty-one persons, but from the bill was deducted a charge of 10s. 6d. for broken glass, which our author, with his accustomed attention to correctness of expression, informs us, was " cordially dissented to."

The Roxburghe Club was extraordinarily convened on the 23rd February 1822, for the purpose of supplying the vacancy occasioned by the death of Mr. George Isted ; upon which occasion Mr. Haslewood pronounces the following homily, in which the reader will remark the judicious accordance of the commencement and the conclusion, besides the singularly refined English in which the whole is conveyed :—

" Well may a weary man in this world, exclaim I am sick of many griefs. Here is an election to record and there must have been a death true Mr. George Isted died   and the vacancy must be filled up. Mr. Isted was a cripple for many years, and though not over full of days, his death was not one of those events that surprise one, and can engender sorrow in the dripping stone. But this entry is made some time after the event that occasions it, and there are others, to which I doubt of doing justice, as I turn over the page more speedy than usual to make the entry, from which every one of the foundation Roxburghers will concede to me that amidst Revels and Hilarity a man may be sick of many griefs.

However, as it is an honour to which I ambitioned, that of making a memorial of the Club, it therefore becomes my duty uncontroulable to give an account of the Dinner Table, though not quite so numerous of guests as at Arthur's Round Table, I brook not Sir Tristram, Sir Lancelot, or a dozen such, but we had lads of right pluck and true courage."

Lord Spencer, Lord Gower, Lord Althorp, Mr. Baron Bolland, &c. were among the " lads of right pluck and true courage," as the elegant annalist words it, and seventeen dined with unusual parsimony for L.25, 14s. Among the party was Mr. Watson Taylor, the new member, chosen in the place of Mr. Isted. Two more deaths occurred before April 13th, when Dr. Dibdin, who, it will be remembered, had been " requested to take the office of Secretary," called the members together to adopt measures to make up for the mortality. " I shall not (says Mr. Haslewood, in one of his best sentences), " quail over it further, but relate a simple fact, which, in a case of sorrow, usually supersedes the best nourished drooping lily that ever flourished in the fertile fields of fancy." Alliteration led him to this flight— above our comprehension certainly. The fact was, nothing more than the rather sudden death, in what our author terms " prematurity of age," of " poor Jemmy Boswell," the son of Dr. Johnson's Biographer, and the editor of the last edition of Shakspeare in 21 vols. The other death was that of Sir Alex. Boswell, in a duel with Mr. Stuart. Mr. Lloyd and Archdeacon Wrangham were elected in their stead, and, after noticing these events, Mr Haslewood adds : " Trusting to the influence which the lettering of this volume, [even the lettering, " Roxburghe Revels," was to have its influence] ought to have, and demanding, as it does, quips and quirks, perhaps it may be remarked, without seeming to want due feeling of preceding events, that

D

perhaps the gloom of the meeting just alluded to might have its origin in what never pleases an Englishman, the want of a dinner." True enough: dinner and wine for the Roxburghers, or even cheerfulness, was out of the question :—those " Lions of Literature" could find nothing worth discussing but turtle and venison, claret and champagne.

Lord Spencer, for some causes not explained, was unable to take the chair on the anniversary, and his son, Lord Althorp, was requested by the Secretary to preside. Now, Lord Althorp had no claim to be considered bibliomaniacal but by descent. He did not feel himself at all qualified for the office of Chairman of the Roxburghe Club, and therefore sent the following reply to the request of Dr. Dibdin :—

" My Dear Sir,

" Our President at the Roxburghe Club should be chosen either from his rank in the state or from his eminence in Bibliomania ; if you take the first as your guide, the Duke of Devonshire should take the chair, if you take the second, I suppose Heber would be the man, but in no possible case ought I to be President. There is indeed another objection to me, which is the high probability which exists that I shall be unable to dine with you at all. There is at present fixed for that day in the House of Commons the Scotch Jury Bill, in the discussion on which I have promised to take a part.

" Believe me yours most truly,

" ALTHORP."

" Albany, June 5, 1822."

The Duke of Devonshire was therefore solicited to preside on the 17th June, 1822, and the expectation that his Grace would take the chair, collected " a goodly company," but as we have already exceeded the limits to which we ought to confine ourselves, we must reserve an account of the proceedings of this day, " so renowned, so victorious," until next week, when we shall insert also the remarkable letter of Sir Walter Scott, in which he consents to accept a seat in the Roxburghe Club, as the representative of the Great Unknown author of the Waverley Novels.

We return to ' The Roxburghe Revels,' and to Mr. Joseph Haslewood, as the author of that immortal record of the proceedings of the " Lions of Literature" who formed the Club.

The Duke of Devonshire had been solicited to preside on the anniversary of the 17th of June, 1822, and the expected presence of his Grace induced twenty-two members to assemble at the Clarendon. Nevertheless, the Duke did not make his appearance, and we applaud his taste. He had probably, seen quite enough of Mr. Haslewood and the " stickers and stayers," or, as the Americans would say, the sitters and squatters, at the celebration of 1816. Lord Morpeth (now Earl of Carlisle) consented to represent the Duke of Devonshire, and he was supported by the following :—

Mr. Dent, Mr. Lang, Sir M. M. Sykes, Mr. Hibbert, Mr. Heber, Mr. Towneley, Mr. Wilbraham, Mr. Bolland, Mr. Drury, Mr. Phelps, Mr. Joseph Littledale, Mr. Bentham, Mr. Utterson, Mr. Carr, Mr. Edward Littledale, Mr. Freeling, Mr. Lloyd, Mr. Ponton, Mr. Markland, Mr. Haslewood, and Mr. Dibdin.

We should like to know whether the members of the Club, in general, were aware of the manner and form in which their proceedings got into the newspapers and magazines. Dr. Dibdin, as we mentioned last week, must have known that his accomplished friend kept a register of all that occurred, and, perhaps, as Secretary (an office which Mr. Haslewood says Dr. Dibdin " requested"), he himself kept another, which hereafter may possibly be brought to auction. If it be, we earnestly advise the then remaining members of the society to purchase it at once, and not to allow it like Haslewood's ' Roxburghe Revels,' to get out into the world, merely because they were unwilling to raise L.50, among them. If we would give L.50, for it, for the sake of printing it, they ought to have been ready to give L.500, for the sake of suppressing it; if only, that people at large might not know how the Club was associated, for what purposes, and under whose auspices. Hereafter, some of the most able and well-informed men, independent of nobility and judges of the land, will always have their names coupled with that of Mr. Haslewood, and *ex uno disce omnes* may be given to them as the motto of the whole association.

We have been led to these remarks by perusing Mr. Haslewood's account of the dinner of June, 1822, in the *Gentleman's Magazine*. The following is the characteristic commencement of his article :—

" A convivial and cloudless anniversary, upheld by a select few, cannot be expected to supply much to amuse, or many events to chronicle ; for the revelry of intellect, though quickened by a sapient banquet, seldom affords much to iterate. The good things must have the energy and raciness of being heard when first delivered, for conversation becomes the bald tale twice told to repeat."

This is a fine specimen of English composition ; not, indeed, exactly worthy of the days of Addison and Swift, but worthy of the Roxburghe Club, and of Mr. Haslewood. " To give a freshness to ancient lore (adds our author,) in each doyley was wrapped *The ordre* of the Tostes ;" and, though we do not clearly see how " ancient lore" could thus obtain any " freshness," we will subjoin them, that our readers may judge for themselves :—

" The immortal Memory of John Duke of Roxburghe—of Christopher Valdarfer, Printer of the Decameron of 1471—of Gutemberg, Fust, and Schoeffher, the Inventers of the Art of Printing—of William Caxton, the Father of the British Press—of Dame Juliana Barnes, and the St. Alban's Press—of Wynkyn De Worde, and Richard Pynson, the illustrious Successors of William Caxton—of the Aldine Family, at Venice—of the Giunta Family, at Florence—The Society of the Bibliophiles, at Paris—The prosperity of the Roxburghe Club—The Cause of Bibliomania all over the World."

We do not wonder that it required some effort on the part of the Roxburghers to gulp down this dry stuff ; and, accordingly, the wine bill amounted to no less than about L.35, out of the L.60, paid to Jacquier. Mr. Haslewood is unusually particular on the occasion, and records " the glorious few" who kept it up like true " peep-o'-day-boys," long after the noble chairman had given notice that he thought it time to separate. The " stickers and stayers" seem to have been Mr. Heber (in the chair,) Mr. Hibbert, Baron Bolland, Dr. Dibdin, Mr. Ponton, and Mr. Haslewood. How fortunate that no " vile compound *partook* of at dinner," or afterwards, pre-

vented our enlighted author from scattering to the last the coruscations of
his wit! No wonder that Baron Bolland could not tear himself away from
this " revelry of intellect, quickened by a sapient banquet." It was, perhaps, this sympathy in taste and feeling which induced Haslewood to dedi-
cate to the Baron his reprint of " Drunken Barnaby's Journal."

But a great event was at hand. We do not allude to the death of Sir M.
M. Sykes, though Mr. Haslewood " lugubriates" (we use a verb of his own
coinage) over his loss in the following strain :—" Carrion Corby still hovers
round our little circle, and again raises his cry in the exultation of the feast
of mortality ; we have lost a man of names and worth." The question was,
how the vacancy was to be filled. On a former occasion, Mr. Haslewood
had given a hint to his friend Mr. Bliss, but it was not taken ; and, if we
are correctly informed, he availed himself of this opportunity to put forward the claims of an individual of very congenial pursuits, and corresponding education : not, indeed, publicly known as an author, but privately recognised as the writer of most of the fulsome puffs that appear in
certain newspapers—a man who (though the trick is now pretty well understood) gets invited to the tables of the great publishers, upon the strength
of the return courtesy in praise and paragraphs—a man who is to be seen
everywhere—at book auctions, where he has a reputation solely on the
score of having formerly bought " in a lump" the collection of an eminent
antiquary, though he himself scarce knows the difference between black-
letter and Roman—at picture sales, where he fastens himself to the skirts
of some connoisseur, or, if there shaken off, upon the arm of some professional dealer—at exhibitions, which he is content to visit in company with a
known critic and wit, who makes him bear his umbrella as well as his
jokes—at theatres, to which free admission is given him, on the express condition that he shall industriously puff the performances in private and in
print—a man who, having no business of his own, has the more time to attend to the business of everybody else, into which he inquires with all the
impertinent effrontery of a cockney Paul Pry, and affects to be " hail, fellow,
well met," with all people of consequence or celebrity, from the Duke of
Wellington down to the little splay-foot American, who has just come to

England to publish his memoirs.   This is the kilderkin of man (not " a tun of man," like Falstaff) who, it was said, was once thought of by Mr. Haslewood as a successor to Sir M. M. Sykes, and who, most assuredly, would have been a competent member of the Roxburghe Club, if in no other respects, so far as regards deglutition and digestion, and putting " *intellectual legs* under mahogany."

However, Lord Spencer and some other influential members had different views, and a special meeting having been called to fill up the vacancy occasioned by the death of Sir Mark M. Sykes, it was attended by fourteen members, including the noble president.   Lord Spencer stated, that a correspondence had been opened with Sir Walter Scott " on the subject of proposing the Author of Waverley, as a proper person to become a member of the Club," and that the following letter had been received from him.   We insert an exact copy of it, because a hurried and incorrect transcript, most likely made secretly when Haslewood's books were on view in Evan's saleroom, *by some such Prying person as the character we have above sketched,* has found its way into the newspapers :—

" My dear Sir,

" I was duly favour with your letter which proves one point against the Unknown Author of Waverly namely that he is certainly a Scotsman since no other nation pretends to the advantage of the Second Sight.   Be He who or where he may he must certainly feel the very high honour which has selected him Nominis Umbra to a situation so worthy of envy.

" As his personal appearance in the fraternity is not like to be a speedy event one may presume he may be desirous of offering some test of his gratitude in the shape of a reprint or such like kickshaw and for that purpose you had better send him the Statutes of your learned body which I will engage shall reach him in safety.

" It will follow as a characteristic circumstance that the Table of the Roxburghe like that of King Arthur will have a vacant chair like that of Banquo at MacBeth's Banquet.   But if this author who ' hath fern-seed and walketh invisible' should not appear to claim it before I come to London (should I ever be there again) with permission of the Club, I who

have something of adventure in me although ' a knight like Sir Andrew
Aguecheek dubb'd with unback'd rapier and on carpet consideration,' would
rather than lose the chance of a dinner with the Roxburghe Club, take upon
me the adventure of the *siege perilous*, and reap some amends for perils and
scandals, into which the Invisible champion has drawn me, by being his Locum tenens on so distinguished an occasion.

" It will be not uninteresting to you to know that a fraternity is about to be
established here something on the plan of the Roxburghe Club but having
Scottish antiquities chiefly in view—It is to be called the Bannatyne Club
from the celebrated Antiquary George Bannatyne who compiled by far the
greatest manuscript record of old Scottish poetry.   Their first meeting is to
be held on Thursday when the health of the Roxburghe Club

" I am always my dear Sir

" Your most faithful humble

Servant

" WALTER SCOTT.

" Edin^r. 25 Feby. 1823"

The cautious wording of this communication, though obviously from its
incomplete termination, hastily written, is well worthy of note; and accuracy in printing it, is the more required, since it is one of the most curious
and interesting relics of a man whose name will stand second only to the
very first authors in our language.   It is worth observing, too, that this
letter was addressed to *Doctor* Dibdin, and *Doctor* he is called in the introduction to ' Quintin Durward;' now, as the reverend gentleman was not
entitled to that honourable appellation until some time after, the coincidence
would have " strengthened other proofs," had Scott not subsequently acknowledged himself the writer of the novels.   The election was of course
unanimous, and the following is Scott's characteristic reply :—

" My dear Sir,

" I am duly honoured with your very interesting and flattering communication.   Our highlanders have a proverbial saying founded on the traditional renown of Fingal's dog.   ' If it is not Bran' they say ' it is Bran's
brother.'   Now this is always a compliment of the first class, whether ap-

plied to an actual cur or parabolically to a biped, and upon the same principle it is with no small pride and gratification, that the Roxburghe Club have
been so very flatteringly disposed to accept me as a locum tenens for the
unknown author, whom they have made the child of their adoption.   As
sponsor I will play my part as I can, and should the Real Simon Pure make
his appearance to push me from my stool why I shall have at least the satisfaction of having enjoyed it.

    They cannot say but what I *had* the crown.

Besides I hope the Devil does not owe me such a shame.   Mad Tom tells
us that the Prince of Darkness is a gentleman, and this mysterious person-
age, will I hope, partake as much of his honourable feelings as of his invi-
sibility, and resuming his incognito permit me to enjoy in his stead an honour, which I value more than I do that which has been bestowed on me by
the credit of having written any of his novels.

  " I regret deeply I cannot soon avail myself of my new privileges, but the
Courts which I am under the necessity of attending officially, set down in a
few days and hei mihi, do not arise for vacation until July.   But I hope to
be in Town next Spring, and certainly I have one strong additional reason
for a London Journey furnished by the pleasure of meeting the Roxburghe
Club.   Make my most respectful compliments to the Members at their next
merry meeting, and express in the warmest manner my sense of obligation.

     " I am always, my dear Sir,

      " Very much

       " Your most obedient Servant

" Abbotsford,   " WALTER SCOTT.

" 1st May 1823

  " Rev^d. D^r. Dibdin

   " Kensington

    " London."

From this day forth, therefore, Sir Walter Scott, representing the Author
of Waverley, was considered a member of the Roxburghe Club; the addition
of his name was sufficient, even to counterbalance the dead-weight of Haslewood, and that is saying a great deal for both.   The last of the two pre-

ceding letters is only a transcript ; we presume, therefore, that Haslewood and Dr. Dibdin divided the spoil, and that as the *first* letter fell to the lot of Haslewood, and was inserted in *his* record of the proceedings of the Roxburghe Club, the original of the *last* letter was reserved by Dr. Dibdin, and may hereafter be found in *his* " Roxburghe Revels," if indeed the learned Doctor has preserved any such register.

What offence the Roxburghe Club had given to Jaquier, is nowhere stated, but he absolutely, and in direct terms, refused to let the members dine at his hotel on the 17th of June 1823. In 1816, he would not treat them as " superlatives," and in 1823 he would not treat them at all ; probably he was quite weary of their dullness and grumbling, or possibly he found his house getting a bad reputation from the vulgarity and ignorance of at least one of the members. The scene of the anniversary of 1823 was, therefore, again transferred to Grillon's, and twenty-one members, with Lord Spencer at their head, sat down to dinner. Archdeacon Wrangham was, for the first time, of the party. " Beyond the chronicle (says Mr. Haslewood, with unusual felicity of phrase,) of the rump-resting by name, and of the rump-rising by numbers, there is little to rehearse. It is true, our vice-president amused the public in a hebdomadal rickety brat, whereof he was one of the pap-supplying nurses during its short existence, with such a blazon of fancy to record the fact of the meeting, that there only remains to give due place to the offspring of his invention."

It should seem that the newspapers and magazines in which the Roxburghers had hitherto puffed themselves, refused, like Jacquier, longer to admit any thing appertaining to the Club ; and Dr. Dibdin having started a ' hebdomadal rickety brat' called *The Museum*, inserted in it some account of the proceedings of the Club on the 17th of June 1823, and did not forget to make an especial note of himself, and of a promised " ORIGINAL work," *by one of the members*, under the title of *the Roxburghe Garland*. This piece of puerility is really not worth farther notice, and we pass over it and Grillon's bill, in order to come the sooner to a real " matter of moment and merriment," (as our author ingeniously words it in his title-page,) though

E

quite unconsciously so by the principal party concerned, and by Mr. Hasle-wood, the narrator of the fact.

One would hardly think, that the son of Dr. Vincent, so long, to our suf-fering, Head Master of Westminster School, and subsequently Dean of the Abbey Church, should be so ignorant as not to know that William Caxton was our first English printer, that he flourished in the reigns of Edward IV. Edward V. Richard III. and Henry VII. and that *he carried on his business in the sanctuary of Westminster.* We owe Dr. Vincent himself such a grudge, that we would willingly find him guilty of this want of knowledge, if, in conscience, we could ; but it is certainly probable that the Chapter was in much the same predicament as the Dean's son, which predicament is appar-ent from the following letter, where he speaks of " the late Wm. Caxton" as of a person who had died the day before. The Roxburghe Club having agreed, as we mentioned in our article of last Saturday, to erect a tablet to the memory of Caxton, had applied to the Dean and Chapter of Westminster, on the subject of a proper situation in the Abbey for fixing it. This was the answer transmitted :—

" Sanctuary Westmr.
21 May 1823.

" Rev^d. Sir,

" I am directed by the Dean, and Chapter, to acquaint you, that neither the situation against the projecting corner by St. Benedict's Chapel, nor on the wall by Shakespear's monument proposed by you to place the Tablet to the late Wm. Caxton are approved, but the space in St. Edmund's Chapel is not objected to, and as soon as you will inform the Dean and Chapter that the Committee acquiesce in the last mentioned situation the Dean and Chapter will consider the price required, of which I will give you due information.

" I am Rev^d. Sir
" Your most obed. serv^t.
" G. G. VINCENT.

" The Rev^d. T. F. Dibdin."

Doubtless, Mr. G. G. Vincent supposed that " the late William Caxton " had been a member of the Roxburghe Club, who was recently deceased ; and it might not occur to him at the moment, that the members of that association, at the rate of two guineas per man, (or per " Lion of Literature,") were about to erect a paltry tablet to a person who had erected such an everlasting monument for himself.   Perhaps, after all, Mr. G. G. Vincent meant his letter as a piece of refined satire, which, in fact, is the best excuse we can make for him. In neither light does the phrase, " the late Wm. Caxton," appear to have struck the members of the Club as anything extraordinary:—

" This day [remarks Mr. Haslewood, of the 17th June 1824, with unwonted bitterness,] reversed all gone before, and the parish Church of St. Margaret's is to be adorned with the monument of Caxton. Voting that the exorbitant Fees of the Abbey sho^d be submitted to was not sufficient, the Goths that guide there, can have no other God than gold : for they gave such a choice of situations that to have followed their sinister wishes wo^d have been not to bury the body, but to bury the monument. A biting satire might be engendered herefrom as ' The Curse of Caxton.' "

The alliteration of " the Curse of Caxton," must have been delightful to our friend, who, when he spoke of " a biting satire," was by no means of opinion that he was not himself capable of writing such a one, as should make an antagonist, like Lycambis of old, go hang himself. Of his imaginary talent in this department, we will give only one brief specimen. When he published one of his reprints, displaying about an equal portion of arrogance and ignorance, it was reviewed somewhere or other with severity. Haslewood found out who was the author of the review, and sent him this " annihilator :"—

To Mr. ——— ———.

You have *no* judgment, and *less* wit
And learning *less than both*—indeed its fit,
If you yourself will please to write a book,
I'll hand it to my culinary cook :
It will do well to bake her *pies on ;*
Poison 'twill be, and not a wise one.

> And thus I answer your long criticism,
> (I'm too good-natured) by a witticism.
> On me your darts can have no force,
> Being armed like a rhinoceros,
> If by you I'm not understood,
> I am your most obedient   J. HASLEWOOD.

This we copy from his own hand-writing—the hand-writing of a " Literary Lion," and a distinguished member of the Roxburghe Club! We wish we had bought that other specimen of his poetical powers, sold among his books, —and yet, what could we have done with such nonsense? As it is, our readers will have had quite enough from his pen, and we will therefore proceed with our narrative.

How the fact is to be explained, we are at some loss to know—whether Jaquier apologized to the Club, or the Club to Jaquier, for the insult of the preceding year—but certain it is, the meeting of the 17th June 1824, was held again at the Clarendon; and as it is admitted that Jaquier's were superior to those of Grillon, and as Jaquier was unusually and personally civil, the chance seems to be, that the difference had been amicably arranged. Our vivacious author's account of the proceedings deserves to be extracted; let the reader " mark the humour of it." Great wits seldom descend to particulars, but Haslewood is an exception.

" About one o'clock, or a wee bit beyond, in the morning of the eighteenth day of June in the year one thousand Eight hundred and Twenty Two ' the Glorious Few' somewhat fevered with the buzz or the bottle of the evening ordered Mr. Jaquier to appear and proceeded to give him a wholesome and fitting (if not sober) lecture upon the subject of the dinner. First the table was too crowded, that was fact the P. & V. P. being each encroached upon to accommodate a member. Second a scarcity of viands, that appeared to be the fact, for no one was satisfied with the Dinner. Third, a member has declared he was hungry then that might be fact, he had taken some trouble to *whet* his appetite. Last. He wanted something to eat then and could not get it, that was nearly the fact, for he ordered dry toast and was told there was *no fire alight* to toast same.—Under these manifold grievances, founded on fact, can it be called a capricious club that we gave notice of quitting to said Mr. Jaquier.—Admitted but (says Will Whipper-in) how haps it that you came back to the old cover. Why because ; now for a Woman's reason, no but it shall be of the same randy, an old proverb ; both bowl down every thing ; therefore because good wine needs no bush.—Grillon's dinner was a better set out, but his wines had not that quickness or raciness which we found at the Clarendon and so we came back, as you see by the interleaved summons.—By this curve in our circle two things were obtained in 1824. Jaquier waited in person during most part of the dinner, ergo, we had mended his manners. The Bill of Fare seemed to satisfy every one, ergo, we had mended the dinner.—And in troth it was so for though the bills of fare of 1822 & 1824 read as nearly similar, they varied marvellously in *fact*. Suffice we are come back again and the ' tarry awhile' sat as usual to rival the ' peep o day boys' in peering for the moon."

Lord Gower presided, and twenty members were present : his Lordship did not quit the chair until a late hour, when, as usual, it was taken by Mr. Heber, and he was supported by the following " stayers and stickers"— Baron Bolland, Sir F. Freeling, Mr Lang, Mr. Hibbert, Mr. Drury, and Dr. Dibdin—Mr. Haslewood does not include his own name among them, nor ' among the drowsy or dead who ordered their palls and departed quietly," and he adds the following paragraph, relating to the extraordinary introduction by Mr. Heber and Dr. Dibdin, of a reverend and learned gentleman, whose name will be familiar to the ears of many. Haslewood observes, that all " the rest," (viz. all but the seven or eight above named,) " went off decently ;" how the " stickers and stayers" went off, whether " decently" or otherwise, is left to inference. We are bad at guessing, and therefore leave it to the reader, after he shall have perused what succeeds :—

" Here the record might have been closed were it not from a circumstance occurring not warranted by precedent and which *may* have a result neither intended or thought of by all parties concerned. At about half past ten, when our mirth seemed near its highest noon, after a short introductory speech from the V. P. and seconded by Mr. Heber (rehearsed before our door opened, by these members) there was admitted to the honour of a sitting that truly bibliomaniacal spirit Mr. Charles Hartshorne.—It is enough here to record the irregularity and hope nothing serious to the abrogation of the Club shall arise from this unexpected breach of privilege."

We are to presume, that our author was present at this singular proceeding (and we call it singular, principally because it was a solitary instance of the kind,) of the Roxburghers, or he would no doubt have told us that he mentioned the fact on the authority of Dr. Dibdin, or some other friend who was in the habit of communicating information to be added to the record preserved under the title of " the Roxburghe Revels."

The old proverb asserts, that " dead men tell no tales," but, as we have already shown, Haslewood has been vastly more communicative since his decease, than he ever was before it ; and if his surviving relations and friends had had any regard for his memory, they ought not only to have burned the MS. before us, but to have carefully erased from every book he possessed, every scrap like a note or remark.   Greater nonsense could not have been written—more rubbish could hardly have been collected.   No event could have brought greater discredit on the members of the Roxburghe Club, and on the lovers of black-letter generally, than the death of Mr. Haslewood, and the consequent exposure.   This, however, it was the duty of those to whom he bequeathed his property to have considered—it does not concern us, and we shall continue the history next week, from the same fruitful source, of " matters of moment and merriment."

Our last notice of this singular, and in many respects, unrivalled, MS., concluded with the introduction to the Club of the Rev. Charles Hartshorne, who never was a member, but who must be known to many of our readers as the editor of a curious volume of Metrical Tales, and of a bibliographical work on the libraries of the University of Cambridge.   A recurrence to this point gives us the opportunity of making one or two observations.   It is to be recollected, that all matters of fact adverted to by us, depend, not upon any knowledge of our own, for we pretend to none, but upon the statements of Mr. Haslewood himself.   We have taken the different assertions, whether they respect persons or events, just as we found them, and we did not purchase the MS. for the sake of any libellous information, it might perchance contain, but simply to afford our readers a little harmless amusement.

For our own parts then, we cannot see the harm of introducing Mr. Hartshorne during one of the protracted sittings of the Club ; and, whether this irregularity were committed by Mr. Heber, then in the chair, or by Dr. Dibdin, the permanent Vice President, or by both, cannot be of the slightest moment. As to the late hours kept by some of the members at their *symposia*, it was a mere matter of taste and discretion ; only, we should not have liked to have been so long condemned to such company. Mr. Haslewood, when at his very best, was not exactly the man to have kept us out of our beds until three or four in the morning.—We will now proceed with the ' Roxburghe Revels.'

It seems that feasting and drinking once a year, and that to no ordinary excess, did not satisfy the appetite and thirst of some of the " Lions of Literature," and, in the first instance, " a *dressed* rehearsal" of the dinner of the 17th of June 1825 was proposed; and, subsequently, the propriety of more frequent meetings in the course of the season was seriously taken into consideration, and a committee formally appointed to decide upon the question. We will go by steps, and first as to the " rehearsal festival," which, of course, was only an excuse for a little more " intellectual guzzling and gormandizing." By whom it was drawn up and issued, does not appear, but a broadside, and, to use our author's expression, " nothing but a broadside," was printed, and sent round in the names of John Fust and William Caxton (whence, possibly, Mr. G. G. Vincent had got his notion, that " the late William Caxton" had been a member of the Club) proposing such a " rehearsal." It was in the following form :—

" 𝕾𝖍𝖆𝖐𝖘𝖕𝖊𝖆𝖗𝖊 𝕻𝖗𝖊𝖘𝖘,
" March ye 9th 1825.

" Maister,
" We grete you wel. Knowe, that divers discrete Members of our beloved Club, called the 𝕽𝖔𝖝𝖇𝖚𝖗𝖌𝖍𝖊, haue made known a fond desire of banqueting togedre, simply and soberly, in utter exclusion of al wines which be

imported from the shores of Gallia—commonlye called Fraunce—(saue and except as is hereafter mentioned) in ordre that such banquetinge may be considered a 𝕽𝖊𝖍𝖊𝖆𝖗𝖘𝖆𝖑 of the great Anniversary Festival of the 17th of June next cominge, now know ye, that should ye be so minded, ye will make known the same by sendinge a messenger, a letter, or by goinge in proper person, to our famed Hotel, called the CLARENDON, where it is intended to establish yᵉ the said REHEARSAL FESTIVAL on Saturdaye the 19th daye of this present moneth, at six of the Clocke, most particularlye.

" And furthermore : Ye shal, if it so convenance, bring thither some curious tome, belike of poetrye, or romaunt-lore, and there displaye the same, to the great ioyance and comfortinge of al eyes whiche thereon loke : And ther shal be no busines done, nor enacted, and eke no lengthened speech-makinge.   But ye are to disport yourself, in simple and pretty discourse, on maters relating to bookes of raritye, choice, or grete coste : and yᵉ meetinge and yᵉ partinge shall be right lovinge.

" A blacke-purple Wine, of insidious tendency, from the shores of Fraunce, shal be permitted to make acquaintance at your handes—on yᵉ finishinge of the Banquete : which shal be also called a " Banquet of Sapience.'

" 𝕴𝖔𝖍𝖓 𝕱𝖚𝖘𝖙
𝖂𝖎𝖑𝖑𝖒. 𝕮𝖆𝖝𝖙𝖔𝖓 } Responsores.

" 𝕻𝖔𝖘𝖙𝖘𝖈𝖗𝖎𝖕𝖙𝖚𝖒.   Ye shall giue notice of such intention of dininge on yᵉ Thursday, the 17th day of yᵉ moneth, precedinge.   If TEN Guestes do not giue such warninge there shal be no such ' Banquet of Sapience.' "

Mr. Haslewood, we dare say, almost with tears in his eyes, registered in red ink, that, though this broadside was " a well-intended publication, it fell a dead letter from the press," and that " no dinner" ! took place in consequence of it.   By what " discreet member" it was prepared, as we have remarked, there is no information, but to make Fust and Caxton date from the " Shakspeare'Press" of Messrs. Bulmer, seems to have been much of a piece with the " simple and pretty discourse," in which each member was invited to " disport himself."   Perhaps some of the graver and more intelli-

gent persons thus addressed did not quite relish the notion of a " right loving meeting and parting" with a man like Mr. Haslewood.

The anniversary was held, as usual, on the 17th of June at Jaquier's, the
Clarendon, and eighteen members were collected, with Earl Spencer at one
end of the table, and Dr. Dibdin at the other. The rest of the names need
not be added, as they were only, as Haslewood would say, the ordinary
" consumers of culinary combustibles." Haslewood tells us, that there was
" no special prosing before dinner, but much was conned after ;" and, as the
whole charge was L.41. 18s., or, L.2. 6s. each, we may conclude that, to the
last, the members entitled themselves to the epithet of " discreet" given in
the above-quoted broadside. On the last occasion, a resolution had been
carried by acclamation, that the Club should not allow any copy of a book,
printed by a member, to be sold for less than L.4. People out of doors began by this time to find out the real worth, or rather the real worthlessness,
of most of the reprints made by the Club; instead of producing from L.10
to L.20 at auctions, they had been sold for L.2 or L.3, and even lower, so
as to disconcert entirely Mr. Haslewood's prudential calculation on the balance in his favour between the cost of a dinner and the price that he could
obtain from Mr. Arch for his Roxburghe Club books. The subject was again
taken up and " conned" after dinner at the meeting of the 17th of June,
1825 ; and, as our author admits, the Club found it impracticable even to
keep up the price of the Club books even to L.4, it was unanimously agreed,
" that the living members should be expected to take care of their own presentation copies, and that those to be protected by the Club should be limited
to such presentation copies as were given by members deceased. Then we
come to a point already touched upon—viz. the anxiety of some of the
" Lions" that their " feeds" should be more frequent.

" It cannot be expected," [says Mr. Haslewood, with his wonted felicity,]
" that the ' Broadside' of such inconvenient registry in this confined volume,
would be shot off without creating some after report. Every one wished to
promote a second or third meeting, and for that purpose a Committee was
named, viz: Mr. Heber—Mr. Phelps—Mr. Dibdin—Mr. Bentham—Mr.
Haslewood—Mr. Bolland to be Chairman : to determine how often the Club

F

should meet in the year, and on what particular days. The first Thursdays in Dec^r. & March and third Thursday in May were to be considered. Winter & Lent circuits to be avoided if possible."

Thus, it is evident that eating and drinking was not only the chief business, but the great point of union of the association. Mr. Haslewood, doubtless, played an admirable knife and fork, if he could do nothing else ; and this, and the high estimation in which his literary attainments must have been held by the Club, amply warranted the selection of him as one of the five to decide how often, and on what days the whole body should assemble. Let the reader here note the extraordinary liberality of the members of the Club : they had never dined together at a less individual cost that L.2, 6s. ; it was now proposed, that they should spend, at least, that sum three times in the year, and yet, with these heavy calls upon their purses, they had been willing to subscribe L.2, 2s. for the erection of a tablet to the memory of the great founder of British typography. This fact deserves record, and we do not think that, in our former papers, we have laid sufficient stress upon it. Let it go down to posterity, that the members of the Roxburghe Club, who had once spent L.5, 14s. each, or L.85, 9s. 6d. upon a single dinner for fifteen persons, were ready to subscribe L.2, 2s. for a tablet to Caxton ! It does not appear, however, that the project of having three dinners in the course of the year, instead of one, was, in the end, brought to bear, although great exertions were certainly made to carry it into effect.

This was the last occasion on which the annual meeting of the Roxburghe Club took place on the 17th of June, the day when the Valdarfer Boccacio was originally put up to auction : nevertheless, the future meetings, whether on the 15th or 31st of May, or on any other day, were still called " anniversaries." But this was a matter of little import, so long as a " gorge " could be obtained at some period or other in the year. On this point, with reference to 1826, Mr. Haslewood remarks, with unusual perspicuousness : " The 17th of June being found such an advance in the season as to force members to absent themselves, *otherwise well disposed to conviviality*, the day was altered to the 2nd, especially as the general election was on the eve of taking place. It was understood, that the day would be earlier than the 17th in future." We then come to some particulars, which we shall give in Mr. Haslewood's own words :—

" No distribution of books, no parish prosing : for the literary world appeared in the last few months to have felt a shock that engendered suspicion and distrust of the most leading bibliopolists and ruin of several minor ones : And we were not without feeling its malignant influence. Another circumstance rife of gossip of a leading Roxburghian served to encrease our gloom though every member present sustained the profound character of a somnambulist and if any one dreampt of the event he did not talk in his sleep. Time may force a further entry to develope the present one until then it may remain unintelligible beyond our circle, for no man is guilty until tried & found so.

" It was determined that no old member sho^d print a book until every one of the present members had given a work and it was intimated to the Vice President that he should write to Mr. Watson Taylor the expectation of the Club that he should present one.

" Mr. Townley proposed indeed moved & it was more than Seconded and Thirded for Two Guineas to be paid in future by every absent member. This was in consequence of the report of an Arch-churchman being seen at an auction on the day of our dinner, who wrote his excuse from the country."

We had intended to pass over the first of these paragraphs without further remark, than that on looking over the MS. with all care, we found no other entry " to develope the present one"; but, upon consideration, it seems to us but justice to the dead, to add, that one who knew Mr. Heber well has often assured us, that, after minute inquiry, carried on from time to time since the report, alluded to by Mr. Haslewood, first obtained circulation, he was satisfied that it never had the slightest foundation. Mr. Heber, he said, was a man of profound, as well as elegant scholarship—a gentleman by nature, as well as by education, but of a mind peculiarly and painfully sensitive, and, like many literary men, without that moral strength which would enable him to meet a calumny of the kind, and which could only be repelled by being courageously encountered. Of the circumstances, we personally know nothing ; but in making this statement, we apprehend we render a more important service to his memory than by seconding any vain attempt to smother the accusation, or pass it over in silence.

On the 2nd of June, 1826, therefore, Mr. Heber was, for the first time, absent from the dinner-table of the Roxburghe Club, to which seventeen members sat down with Lord Spencer, Lord Gower, Mr. Justice Littledale, &c. The noble chairman does not seem to have retired quite so early as usual, and at his departure Mr. Bolland succeeded to his presidential chair. But why should not our illustrious historian, in his own matchless and figurative language, let the reader into the secrets of the *symposium ?* " The skirmishers (says Mr. Haslewood) that took parol, without pattern of the commander-in-chief, were Lord Gower, Mr. Carr, Mr. Phelps, Mr. Justice Littledale, Mr. Edward Littledale, and, in due time, Earl Spencer, when there was elected for his depute, Mr. Bolland, whose vivacity, being afloat with the coruscating spirits around him (except the evaporating staid ones, Mr. Hibbert and Mr. Ponton), served to give a further medley to time, and tarried us to near the break of morning." Happy language ! Happy Haslewood ! and happy Roxburghers, to have had such a registrar of your revelries ! Alexander wept over the tomb of Achilles, because he, " the great Emathian conqueror," had no such poet as Homer to immortalize his victories. If he had had but a Haslewood, he would have spared his tears—but the world would have lost one of the sweetest sonnets of the sweetest of Italian versifiers.

" Dent and Dulness" died at the close of 1826 : the last time he dined with the Club was on the 17th of June, 1824. If Mr. Dent were not a very bright man—if he were not exactly one of the " coruscating spirits" that Mr. Haslewood calls himself and others, who remained drinking till daybreak on the 2nd of June 1826, he was a gentleman, and since he wrote the first article on these " Revels," we have been assured, on good authority, that Haslewood's alliterative censure, above quoted, arose, as we suspected, from a slight shown by Mr. Dent to Haslewood in not acknowledging him " the wizard of the south," as Sir Walter Scott had been designated " the wizard of the north." To those who are ignorant of Haslewood's egregious vanity and overweening estimate of himself, this will appear impossible; but we are assured that the fact is so, and we can almost believe it. However this may be, a meeting was called for the 5th of March, in order to fill the vacancy occasioned by the death of Mr. Dent ; and, of course, the vacancy in the stomachs of the members. No difficulty was experienced in either operation : the Hon. and Rev. G. Neville Grenville did the one, and Jacquier the other ; but, a very uncomfortable clause was inserted in the hotel keeper's note of invitation, which ran thus :—" It is afterwards proposed to dine on a reduced scale of expense, at seven o'clock." The reader may imagine the result : only fourteen out of the thirty-one members could be collected, and Lord Spencer took his chair unsupported by Mr. Haslewood! This " coruscating spirit" had vanished at the very notion of a cheap dinner for the Roxburghe Club, and he records, that the account of what transpired on this occasion was furnished to him by his " accurate friend, G. H. Freeling, Esq."

It will be remembered, that the purchase of the Valdarfer Boccacio by the Marquis of Blandford, (now Duke of Marlborough), having been the origin of the Roxburghe Club, he became a member of it, but had never yet dined with the association. It seems that his Grace had intended to have joined the party on the 5th March 1827, but hearing that the dinner was likely to be, in *Haslewoodian* phraseology, " cheap and nasty," " his Grace (says our ' coruscating' Reveller) sent a message by Lord Spencer, that he would have attended, but was compelled to go to Blenheim, as this day. His Grace found fault with the letter of invitation, as he did not admire a cheap and inferior dinner." Let it not be forgotten, that those who now ordered " a cheap and inferior dinner" at the Clarendon, were the very gentlemen who had complained some time before, that Jaquier did not " treat them as superlatives." No wonder our " superlative" Haslewood and the Duke of Marlborough stayed away, and left the revelry " for this night only," to Lord Spencer, Mr. Bolland, Mr. Freeling, and the *&c.* of the Club. Haslewood denounces it, on the authority of his " accurate friend," as a " most trumpery concern, which had but one defender, the Vice President, who was rather feverish thereon." Let us see what the Vice President himself says upon the subject in a note to Haslewood, most fortunately preserved in the volume before us. We print it with all its emphatic italic :—

" Dear H.   " March 8

" I can't stir from my neighbourhood, having too many engagements, with *knives* and *forks,* to dispense with.

" I *long* to *see* you— to tell you of the most *extraordinary* meeting, in *all* respects, which ever took place at the Clarendon : a part of which extraordinary work, is, the villainously *meagre* dinner—and yet we had L.1 17s. each to pay.

" Your *chronicling* powers were much needed. *I* will attempt *something :* A hot skirmish betn Markland, Utterson, and myself on *one* side—& Bolland & H. Freeling on the other ; President interfered !   " T. F. D."

Either Haslewood had been misinformed when he asserted that the dinner was defended by the Vice President, or Dr. Dibdin had changed his opinion of it between the 5th and 8th March. Certain it is, that the Club did not again assemble at the Clarendon, and by reason of the general dissatisfaction of the members. The meeting, it seems, on Dr. Dibdin's authority, was " most extraordinary," and it is hardly to be wondered, under the circumstances, that he regretted the absence of his friend, (whom he *longed* to *see*' —what a taste !) whose " *chronicling* powers were much needed." We have the satisfaction of finding, however, that Dr. Dibdin had resolved " to attempt something" of the kind himself, and we presume that sooner or later it will be brought to light. As the failure of this extra-feed of the 5th March, is a great event in the annals before us, the reader may like to see the bill of fare, which was pronounced " a most trumpery concern," and is so registered upon the document itself :—

First Course.

Soups à la Reine.   Rice.

Fish Crimp'd Cod.   Fillets of Soles
                                     Tanagou sauce.

Removes   Loin of Veal à La Bechamel.

Ham.

Entrees Fricassée & Chickens à la Chevaliere

Vole au vent with a Ragout Melée

Hachis de Volaille á La Polonaise

Mutton Cutlets with Harrico beans.

Second Course.

Roasts   Capons   Larks.

Entremets   Jelly.

Fried Celery.

Macaroni.

Pastry.

Charlotte.

Blanc Mangé.

For this, with the wine, we have seen by Dr. Dibdin's note, L.1, 17s. per head was charged : how much of the " red, red juice " was consumed, we have unluckily no information, but as the " hot skirmish " was carried so far as to require the interference of the noble President, we may presume that the parties engaged at least had partaken of it pretty abundantly.   In the abstract, therefore, the bill does not seem to us to have been immoderate. At this meeting, a resolution was adopted of some importance.   It became every day more apparent, that if publications were only left to the members of the Club, the books, instead of obtaining high prices by auction, would soon be sold at a loss, in consequence chiefly, of the bad selection of subjects, in which even the members could take little interest.   Mr. Hibbert, there-fore, proposed, for the purpose of keeping up the character of the Club, that a MS. of general interest and intrinsic value, as illustrative of manners, institutions, or literature, should be selected and printed at the joint expense. The suggestion was adopted directly, and Lord Spencer, Mr. Bolland, Mr. Utterson, Mr. Markland, Mr. Phelps, and Dr. Dibdin, were constituted a committee to consider of the fit mode of carrying the object into effect.

We had hoped to be able to finish with the " Roxburghe Revels " in our present number ; but we have a good deal to say (and so has Mr. Haslewood) upon the above resolution, and the manner in which it was carried into effect, under the care of Mr. (now Sir Frederick) Madden : we must, there-fore, defer it and more until next week, when we think we and the rest of the world will have done with Mr. Haslewood for ever. We shall then also give his account of the only dinner of the Club, at which Sir Walter Scott, as the representative of the author of ' Waverley,' was present.

Mr. Haslewood and the Roxburghe Club will receive their *coup de grace* this week ; and we shall be most happy to have done *with*, as well as done *for*, both.

We are heartily sick of the detail of mere sensual indulgence, and shall hereafter touch as little as possible upon the gormandizing propensities of the Roxburghers. We cannot, however, omit all reference to the subject, inasmuch as we have undertaken to give an account of the proceedings of the Club, and eating and drinking appears to have been with them the *rerum omnium primum*—the " be all, and the end all "—in proof, having cast our eyes once again over the different tavern bills, we find, that since its first institution, up to the date at which we are now arrived, 1826, " the Lions of Literature " had spent upwards of a L.1000 upon feeding and guz-zling only. In addition, however, they had laid out L.2, 2s. upon a tablet to the memory of Caxton !

Jaquier being, apparently, in eternal disgrace for the " trumpery concern" mentioned in our last, and Grillon and others having probably refused to *take in* the Club any longer, a move, or (to speak technically, like our au-thor's " culinary cook") a *remove* was made to Freemason's Tavern, and Mr. Cuff agreed to give " a three-course dinner off plate," to include turtle and dessert, at a guinea per head, calculating, we suppose, upon making up his loss by the wine. Haslewood—in a passion of enthusiasm on this occasion—breaks out into poetry :—

> Brave was the banquet, the red red juice,
>   Hilarity's gift sublime,
> Invoking the heart to kindred use,
>   And bright'ning halo of time.

He does not, however, furnish any information as to the actual cost of this " brave banquet," only observing, that " every one appeared gratified and satisfied," but adding, that " the record of particulars of the *grub* and the guinea" must be reserved to a future occasion. Had he inserted the particulars, we should have omitted them, in order that we might advert more in detail to the steps taken by the Club regarding the publication of the highly curious and intrinsically valuable poem ' Havelock the Dane.'

Experience had proved over and over again that the reprints made by the members of the Club, and under their own superintendence, with a very few exceptions, were worth nothing—that they were mere waste paper, and paper wasted. Sir F. Madden (then Mr. Madden, and Conservator of the MSS. in the British Museum) was dining with Lord Spencer, when the resolution of the Club, adopted at the previous anniversary, was brought under discussion; and Sir F. Madden mentioned, that he had recently discovered the long-lost poem of ' Havelock the Dane' in the Bodleian Library. It immediately struck Lord Spencer and some other members of the Roxburghe Club, who were present, that it was exactly the sort of thing that was wanted; and a Committee having been appointed to take the subject into consideration, they resolved in the affirmative, and at the " anniversary ' of the 31st of May, 1827, it was proposed and agreed, that ' Havelock the Dane' should be printed, and that the impression, instead of being like the Club books, confined to thirty-five copies, should be extended to eighty. Here, therefore, were symptoms of improvement in the nature and value of the work to be printed—in the enlargement of the means of circulation—and

G

in the choice of the person who was to have the care of the undertaking. It was agreed that the whole should be intrusted to Sir F. Madden: and now let us insert what our distinguished author of the ' Roxburghe Revels' says upon the subject.   He disliked the innovation; and, above all, he disliked that a person, who was not a member of the Club, should be employed to superintend the impression.   It is clear that Haslewood had hoped for the editorship himself, notwithstanding his notorious and glaring incompetence, and did not attend any of the meetings, in the expectation that he would be fixed upon; well knowing that, if he were present, such a proposition could hardly, with any regard to delicacy, be made.

" *Havelock the Dane.*"

" The entries on this subject will be as brief as propriety admits in an historical narrative.   The printing of Havelock the Dane, if planned to enlarge was not completed to sustain the character of the Club; that is if its literary character may be believed something more than fancied and having virtual existence.   To the point :—Thirty one members having run the round of each selecting and printing some particular work finally agree to select and print ' a MS. of general interest' at the expense of the Club : to accomplish this—what was the expedient ? A MS. not discovered by a Member of the Club, was selected and an excerpt obtained, not furnished by the industry, or under the inspection of any one Member ; nor edited by a Member—but in fact after much pro and con, it was made a complete hireling concern, truly at the expense of the club, from the copying to the publishing. If the doubt which naturally presents itself, (looking at the public reputation of each member, as a literary man) whether every one was not indebted to auxiliary aid (as essential but excepting the printer) in the individual presentments can be parried by the fact of labours well known, an enquiry might arise as to the want of volunteer assistance in such an emergency to sustain the character of the club and shield it from the imputation of either indolence or impotency.—All slunk from a task, it must be supposed, that should have excited the cupidity of every member.—Those who sanctioned seemed entirely to forget the important semblance of the club, not willing, it is friendly to presume, to incur any labour, or responsibility.—A portion of the Absentees from the meetings held on this matter could not consistently from residence be present, while others voluntary absent may be found among those who value the honour of being a Member highly always provided, it demands no labour. The remainder of the 31 might absent from the bye meetings as knowing it not possible to stem wind and tide (especially if the first ruleth the latter) or to drop a proverbial apposite P. & V. P. —Suffice—the end thrust as an appropriate lodgment, the notorious club of *Bibliomaniacs* into a MAD—DEN. To effect this the Committee appointed 31st May 1827 recommended the printing of Havelock the Dane & a meeting held 31st May following, present Earl Spencer, Duke of Devonshire, Lord Althorp &c. &c. adopted certain resolutions not afterwards acted upon. A general meeting required by circular dated 1st Febr^y 1828 for Thursday the 7^h at which was present Earl Spencer, T. Ponton, W. Bentham, J. H. Markland, E. V. Utterson, Esq^res. and the Rev. D^r. Dibdin who passed seven propositions to submit to a fuller attendance of the Members on Tuesday the 19th. On the latter day was present Earl Spencer, Earl Gower, The Hon. & Rev. N. Grenville, Rev. W. H. Carr, G. Hibbert, T. Ponton, E. V. Utterson, J. H. Markland, W. Bentham, Esq^res. & Rev D^r. Dibdin, who unanimously resolved in the course of Eleven resolutions, to give to William Madden Esqre. of the B. Museum L.100 for editing—that each Member pay for his own copy L.6. 6.—& for an extra copy L.2. 2.—On the 25th of Oct. following obtained my copy, but the printed circular was not dated until the 4th Nov^r.—It ought to have been delivered at the meeting of the club next narrated & the entry here of time of delivery out of chronological order, is to dismiss a subject of which it is hoped no similar one will find sanction hereafter from the Club."

Here we see the Haslewood shine out in all his mild lustre : his mind was a perfect moonbeam, from its purity and its brightness. We have no inclination to comment on this quotation ; but, just let the reader imagine a man who could so write, selected to be the editor of a work which required a knowledge, not only of English, but of Greek, Latin, German, old French, and Anglo-Saxon. Why, even the Roxburghe Club could not so grossly blunder as to appoint him; and, from his non-appointment, proceeded his disappointment. He gave vent to his vexation in the paragraphs we have cited, and he, moreover, stirred up a man, a little abler than himself (where could he find an inferior?), to put together some hasty "remarks" upon Sir F. Madden's Glossary to 'Havelock the Dane,' which remarks, in some respects, seemed a happy imitation of Haslewood. He had hoped that his friend's "Remarks" would make Sir Frederick as mad as Dennis had been driven by the 'Re-remarks upon Cato'; and it was certainly no proof of sanity that Sir Frederick condescended to answer. We have said thus much about 'Havelock,' because it is a work which, on the whole, does credit to the Club, and the Club has need of something to do it credit.

We give the body no praise for the election of Sir Walter Scott: he was a known lover of literary antiquities, besides being the first author of the age, and there could not be a moment's hesitation in the choice. What must strike every one who knew our friend, or has read these papers, is the strangeness of the association of such men as "the Wizard of the North" and our would-be "Wizard of the South." But we will pass this point, and proceed to the celebration of the 15th of May, 1828, at which Sir Walter Scott was for the first, and last, time present. He had quite enough of it: one day perfectly satisfied him; for, although he met on that occasion Earl Spencer, the Duke of Devonshire, Lord Althorp, Lord Clive (elected of the Club on May 1st), Mr. Phelps, Mr. Markland, Mr. Towneley, and other accomplished gentlemen, Haslewood seems to have been a sort of "frog in the fire," or a wet blanket which cast a damp over the whole company: his uninformed dullness was like a cloud that overshadowed and oppressed. And here we must notice a peculiarity in the arrangement of the guests at table. Earl Spencer was in the chair, with the Duke of Devonshire on his right, and Sir Walter Scott on his left. Haslewood also sat to the right of the President, but it is singular that nobody would sit near him on the same side; and rather than do so, Mr. Markland and Mr. Ponton ranged themselves opposite, and thus destroyed altogether the equilibrium of the table. Everything shows that our friend was rather endured than liked: the wonder is, how he could be endured.

After assigning some reasons why only eighteen sat down to dinner, and mentioning that Sir Walter Scott had exhibited a work intended for distribution among the members, Haslewood thus, in his own inimitable style, describes the proceedings of the day :—

" The viands at three crowns per head only, the wine ad valorem, might have satisfied a crown'd head, though of mere passive importance in life. If good viands please the mind and good wine gladdens the heart, their powers of exhilerating are easily diminished, a slight indisposition or a temporal anxiety in worldly events ever tyrannise over cheerfulness and society, however select, cannot conquer however it may slightly ameliorate a depression of spirits. Our President laboured under the effect of a severe cold, and the giant of the North had his power of amusement damped by the incertitude of the event of the dangerous illness of his grandson. These apparently personal matters may be minuted as a reason for the record seeming scanty, and of lesser importance than usual, considering who were present. A modified system seemed to arise from these circumstances, and the conversation was in a more softened tone than customary at a convivial party, and after a gentlemanly parlance of rather more than three hours, the Duke having gone to the King's ball, and others of the Upper House departed, the bill was called and exit."

It is very clear that " the Giant of the North" was grievously disappointed with his company, but it is quite as clear that Haslewood, " the Giant of the South," was disappointed too : a " modified system seemed to arise," and " the conversation was in a more softened tone than customary at a convivial party :" he means, of course, at a convivial party of Roxburghers, which, to use his own words on a former occasion, usually " combined all that Anacreon was famed for, tempered with the reason of Demosthenes, and intersected with the archness of Scaliger." We will not give our own interpretation of these expressions, nor say how much noise, vulgarity, or obscenity, were absent on the occasion to which we are now alluding, when Haslewood regrets that " viands at three crowns per head," and " wine, ad valorem," although, generally, " good viands please the mind [of a Roxburgher], and good wine gladdens the heart," failed to make Lord

Spencer, the Duke of Devonshire, Sir Walter Scott, Lord Althorp, Lord Clive, and others, forget themselves in coarse carousings and obstreperous mirth. It is not unlikely that Sir Walter Scott was little disposed to converse unreservedly, and that the most capable members were influenced by the same feeling ; but, it is not unlikely also, or, rather, it is most probable, that Haslewood could not understand half that was said, and could not recollect the half that he understood. We think that some of the other members present, such, for instance, as Mr. Markland, or Archdeacon Wrangham, could have given a very different version of the day's proceedings. We hope, indeed, that some better record has been preserved, and that Mr. Lockhart, when he publishes the promised Life of his father-in-law, will not be obliged to insert such trash as we have quoted.

The dinner was one of the most economical ever partaken of by the Club, the whole charge for eighteen members being only L.38. ; whereas, when only fifteen, without a title among them, dined at the Albion in 1818, the charge, it will be remembered, was L.85. The Club-books were at a heavy discount in 1828, and Haslewood, balancing profit and loss, was content with moderate fare, and without being considered a " superlative." The tone of the whole Club was now lowered.

One proof of this alteration is the re-condescension of the Roxburghers to dine at the Clarendon on June 23, 1829 ; for, though Mr. Cuff had given great satisfaction on two occasions, Freemasons' Tavern was not looked upon as a genteel resort (at least so says Haslewood, whose judgment in all matters of *bienséance* is indisputable) by some of the members ; and it was thought a less indignity again to beg Jaquier's pardon, than to be guilty of visiting Great Queen Street. Haslewood was in one of his most sprightly veins, when he wrote as follows :—

" What Clarendon Hotel again. And by what chance came you there once more ?—I am not a Free-Mason. The majority of those societies smatter much of the tap tub. The title and mistificated insignia never *aspires* above handicraft classes and a sentiment of this description prevails sufficiently in Society to have an effect somewhat prejudicial to the tenant of the Freemason's Tavern.—It was discovered that in our very limited circle more than one member, absolutely objected and indeed mentioned their determination of never dining with the Club while the Meetings were held at that Tavern. The objection appeared strange and hardly to be credited, but by chance I discovered a Member that had expressed such determination to the V.P. He described the House as of an inferior character, and unfit to be the haunt of gentlemen. This opinion seems to originate in the Hall being a place for meetings of Freemasons, and however policy enlinks a few leading characters to take ostensible situations at Grand Meetings, there is not sufficient in the gilding to pass the common alloy into currency.—Be it as it will our V.P. once and again installed us at the Clarendon.

" Nothing singularly luxuriant to characterise the dinner, though something of novelty might have been reasonably expected to hail our return. It was bespoke for 14.—After Lord Spencer left the Chair, a rally round Bolland and a fresh bottle quickened the tarrying Spirits to mirth and good fellowship and all would have passed in good keeping but unfortunately the appetite vamped up a claim to something eatable and a ' broiled bone ' became the object needed and what so easy to obtain at a Tavern.—Ring the bell—Give the order—To the astonishment of all present, lo, the old answer ' No Fire alight.'—It is alleged that some men benefit by experience, Mr. Jaquier appears an exception."

The fact seems to be, that Jaquier might now do what he liked with the humbled Club, especially as the dinner bill had been so cut down as to amount to only L.33. 4s. They had been driven about from pillar to post, and from post to pillar : " the world was all before them," and *nowhere* " to choose," so that they were compelled to put up with the accommodation Jaquier thought fit to give them. This remark will equally apply to the anniversary of 12th of May, 1830, and the members had been taught better than at 12 o'clock at night to require an anchovy toast ; " no hue and cry (says our author) after a broiled bone." The President, and the most distinguished members of the Club, of course, knew nothing of the airs Jaquier gave himself, and the whole affair seems to have been managed between Dr. Dibdin and Haslewood. Either they had some private reasons for adhering to Jaquier (we mean nothing offensive), or they found nothing objectionable or unusual, so far as they were concerned, in the insolence of an hotel-keeper. They seem to have been used to it.

For brevity, we have always called the annual meetings of the Club anniversaries, on whatever day they might be held, but the inconvenience of constant changes in this respect having been felt, a resolution had been adopted on the 8th of June, 1829, that the dinner should always take place on the first Thursday in May. Nevertheless, it was not adhered to on the very first occasion, and the assembly of 1830 took place on Wednesday, the 12th of May. Mr. Phelps, for some reason or other, could not then attend, and Mr. Bentham being a musical " Lion" (like that celebrated in the German Popular Tales), and a subscriber to the Antient Concerts, preferred to treat his ears rather than his palate, especially as Jaquier was again to provide. Haslewood laments the changes in the days of dining; for, as he sagely observes, " in all the ventures of life, certainty is the most eligible," especially the certainty of getting or going without a dinner, and we cannot resist the pleasure of quoting the following character of Dr. Dibdin from his immortal pen. We are sure that the Doctor will feel much obliged to his lamented friend for having left it upon record, that he is " as lively as a lark, as restless as a squirrel," and that he " seldom appears to imbibe an opinion staid and absolute." To Dr. Dibdin, Haslewood imputes the vacillation we have mentioned.

" Such a succession of comparative uncertainty is enough to mar the meetings of any Society and in particular one predisposed to be well regulated and acting upon certainty, for in all the ventures of life certainty is the most eligible. Unfortunately the record has one in appearance of anything but bearing that character. To attempt to fix blame would be invidious otherwise our volatile V. P. might be found the founder of the error (if it is one) as he seldom appears to imbibe an opinion staid and absolute, such as can live thro' years. Lively as a lark, restless as a squirrel; always in high spirits (even to the envy of those around him,) and therefore seldom considering of results and ever believing he thinks right, from undeviating rectitude of thought, concludes all must be right as far as he is concerned. I note this fearing the error has *shook* the foundation of the Roxburghe Club.

Our illustrious annalist's grammar and spelling are both conspicuous in this choice extract, and we never shall cease to wonder how it was possible for the rest of the Club to associate upon any terms with such a mass of ignorant presumption. This is a question we have asked before, and we should like to have it answered. What on earth had Haslewood to recommend him? We can discover in a moment why the company of a man like the Rev. E. C. Hawtrey, a gentleman, a scholar, one acquainted with many European languages, and with a mind stored from all sources of knowledge, should be eagerly sought, and we are not surprised, therefore, at his election in June, 1831, to fill the vacancy on the death of the Rev. W. Holwell Carr; but here again, how was it possible to put Mr. Hawtrey in contact with Haslewood? If not forewarned, how he must have stared on the anniversary of the 24th of May, 1832, the first he attended, to hear the latter open his mouth. But, as Haslewood would say, and has said, comparisons are "invid*uous*."

Haslewood seems to have been in high spirits on the 3rd of June, 1831: again he breaks out with his favourite stanza, before quoted, "Brave was the banquet," &c., but in a moment of serious reflection, he adds, "Gay may be the glass, still the unreading reader, allowed to peruse [what a privilege!] this inconsequential [he always uses this word in the sense of unimportant] chronicle, would unquestionably be surprised to find any excitement beyond dullness [note the phrase, "unreading reader," "any excitement *beyond dullness*,"] could be derived from our usual customary [a poetical pleonasm] and, in part, obsolete toasts." So far as we can make out his meaning, we are very much inclined to agree with him: we inserted a list of the toasts in our last article. "Our dinner (he observes farther on) had been *bespoke* for fifteen, and we squatted to number, and retired minus fifty shillings each. Our dinner was a guinea a head, and the divisible proportion of our libations is scarcely worth min*a*ting."

"Only eleven—few—lamentable few! but not without arbitrary reasons," are the words with which our gifted author opens his brief narrative of the

H

proceedings at the anniversary of the 24th of May, 1832—who were the "lamentable few" who still were willing to belong to a club in which Haslewood had a seat? Lord Clive was in the chair, owing to the indisposition [to come?] of Lord Spencer, and he was supported by the Rev. Mr. Hawtrey, the lately elected candidate, Mr. Ponton, Mr. Utterson, Mr. Markland, Mr. Justice Littledale, Mr. Towneley, Mr. Phelps, Mr. Bentham, Mr. Haslewood, and Dr. Dibdin. These may be considered the last of the Roxburghers: for, although a meeting of a similar kind was held in 1833, we are without any register of its proceedings. " All expressed (says our author) regret and lamentation, but is it to be fancied real or unreal?" This is a " shrewd doubt," and the fact certainly was, that very few, perhaps no one, with the exception of Haslewood, was sorry that the Roxburghe Club should die a natural death. " That (viz. whether the regret was real or unreal) is not my task to opiniate upon or unravel; suffice, there is a brief notice of the fact, and our travel is somewhat too fast, for there is not upon record yet the covetable burst of the Lion of the day from Lord Cawdor, in the print of ' William and the Werwolf,' got up under the editorship of Mr. Madden."

We ought, in the regular course of events, to have mentioned before, that Lord Cawdor had been elected in June 1829, on the death of Mr. Roger Wilbraham, and with laudable zeal he immediately set about reprinting for the Club, the remarkable poem of ' William and the Werwolf,' to which attention had previously been drawn by the Reverend Mr. Hartshorne, in his ' Metrical Tales.' In order that the whole might be done in the best manner, his Lordship resorted to Sir F. Madden, who had so well discharged his editorial duty, in the instance of ' Havelock the Dane,' though Mr. Haslewood and his friend *(habet et musca splenam, et formica sua bilis inest)* had carped at it. By this time, they both seem to have discovered their error, and however Haslewood might grudge at the selection of Sir F. Madden, by Lord Cawdor, when he thought (poor deluded creature!) that he himself had preferable claims, he was too prudent to make his dissatisfaction public, and in the record in our hands he has only registered the bare fact of preference. ' William and the Werwolf ' was the very last book printed by

any member of the Club, before its extinction, (for it is extinct, and Haslewood has extinguished it,) and it does the body to the full as much credit, perhaps, as any other production which it countenanced   We may say, therefore,
of the Roxburghe Club in this expiring act, under the auspices of the Thane
of Cawdor, what Shakspeare says of the Thane of Cawdor himself;

> Nothing in his life
> Became him like the leaving of it.

If the Roxburghe Club had but commenced upon the plan with which it
concluded, viz. applying its funds to the printing of manuscripts, or to the
reprint of works the value of which had been ascertained and decided upon
by others, we could almost have found in our hearts to forgive them all their
exclusive foppery.   To multiply a unique copy of a valuable work to thirty-
five, or, as in the case of ' Havelock the Dane,' to eighty impressions, is at
least so far a gain.

We are now drawing very near the conclusion of the MS. of ' The Roxburghe Revels,' and notwithstanding the offensive ignorance of the writer,
there is something so ludicrous about his self-importance, and something so
laughably absurd in his style, that we almost regret to be so near the end of
our labours.   At one moment, we feel heartily weary of our task, and in the
next we stumble upon a passage, an anecdote, or an incident that in one way
or other seems to compensate for all our trouble.   The following is the last
line we shall quote from this notorious volume, and it is highly characteristic : the bad grammar, the conceit, the affectation of humour and sprightliness, and withal the vulgarity, are equally conspicuous :—

" Such trifles on such occasions *tells* well and *gives* a fillup to the evening
lucubration.   Notwithstanding our paucity of number we were friendly
without argument, jocose, lively, and consistent.   There was no seeming
hero of the table, and therefore no one injudiciously loquacious : A complaint perhaps less to be advanced as against the R. Club, than any collec-
tive party I was ever in.—To be short there is to conclude the day the bill
of fare to introduce ; As why ? M. Jaquier has retired to his foreign domain
and common consistency demands in what manner we are now catered for,

and certainly the best (if not very best) dinner I have partaken of at the Clarendon : But let the Clerk of the Kitchen exhibit his own spurious dialect."

These few lines contain, as it were, the essence of Haslewood : the allusion " to the seeming hero of the table," was a hit at Sir Walter Scott, and shows the paltry envy of our Roxburgher's character.   People may talk as they will of the envy of actors and artists, but it is nothing compared with the envy of authors of an inferior grade : your low *litterati* form the most grudging, carping, fretting, and in some respects most mischief-making and malignant, class of the community.   We see it increase in proportion as we descend the scale : Shakspeare, Milton, and Walter Scott, could not be envious ; but Ben Johnson, Dryden, and Pope had a spice of it ; it corroded the hearts of Ralph and Hill, it was the death of Duck, (we allude to Stephen of that name) ; it turned to curds all the ' milk of human kindness," of the poetical retailer of sky-blue in Bristol,* and it devoured Haslewood.   It is really laughable to find such a man, after penning such a specimen as the above, talking slightingly of the " spurious dialect" of Mr. Chaplin's (for Jaquier had relinquished the Clarendon) clerk of the kitchen.   How the waiters could have kept their countenances, while attending upon the Roxburghers, when Haslewood opened his mouth, we cannot imagine.   Although Jaquier would never treat him as such, he really was, in his way, a " superlative."

But the Roxburghe Club had not yet reached the lowest point of its declination.   With one exception, the constant Vice President had been Dr. Dibdin, a man, as his friend Haslewood says, " volatile, lively and restless," and he proved his friendship by saying no more.   The Doctor, it seems, was absent on the anniversary of the Society which was held in the beginning of May 1833 ; the last it ever celebrated, and the last it will ever celebrate. It was necessary, therefore, to supply his absence ; and who does the reader imagine was the distinguished individual who was " pressed" to become the Doctor's deputy ?   No other than our friend Joseph, author of the ' Roxburghe Revels' !   Lord Spencer was not in his place as President, and we know not who was in the chair, for here our record unhappily fails us ; it closes with the account of the meeting of 24th of May 1832.   We said that

---

* Anne Yearsley, the Poetical Milk-Maid.

the quotation, made two paragraphs above, should be the last specimen we would insert of the literary labours of our renowned author, but we cannot refuse a place to his last memorable words, consisting as they do of a most choice original couplet, struck off in the heat of the moment. Wordsworth maintains that poetry is not an immediate, but a reflected impression; and Haslewood proves the truth of the position; for next day, casting back his thoughts to the dinner, wines, &c. of the preceding night, and remembering the satisfaction they had diffused, he again bursts into song—" The Champaigne was excellent; the Port superior! Then who can doubt of

> " Choice Cates and good wines promoting hilarity,
> And the Revels last close, dear conviviality ! ! "

And here we should close, with " the Revels last close," since " the force of nature can no farther go," were we not anxious to preserve to the world and to posterity the very latest specimen of the composition of one so cherished, while living, by every Roxburgher, and whose memory, now he is dead, will be cherished by unborn generations. We have stated that Haslewood occupied the Vice-presidential seat at the anniversary of 1833, and, slipped into the volume before us, is a scrap of paper, containing the rough draught of a letter he sent to Lord Spencer, informing him of certain nominations which had been made to fill up certain vacancies. And here we may note the trait in Haslewood's characte , (trifles are important when they relate to great men,) that he never seems to have penned the most casual note, without having first made a rough copy, so that it is quite clear that all the extracts we have made from the Roxburghe Revels, were the results of much thought and patient correction. We wish we had time to have the letter to Lord Spencer lithographed, but we must be content to give it intelligibly in type, only remarking that Haslewood seems, by the difference of handwriting, to have employed some person to aid him in the correction of it, before he copied it fair for transmission to Earl Spencer.—

" Conduit Street 11th May 1833.

" My Lord,
" Having been pressed at the late meeting of the Roxburghe Club to act deputy for our much regretted absentee, the V. P., I believe it is my duty

to communicate to your Lordship that after dinner the subject of the present vacancy in the Club, by the lamented death of Sir Walter Scott being discussed, the following nominations of candidates for such vacancy were made : Mr. Baron Bolland proposed Mr. B. Barnard of Ham Common Surrey ; Lord Clive proposed Mr. Archdeacon Butler of Shrewsbury,—I have, &c."

Now, here we have only to observe, that among other peculiarities, before the rough draft was corrected, it stood " the following nominations of candidates *was* made," consistently with our friend's usual non-observance of the trammels of " grammar rules."   However, Lord Spencer must have been used to this disregard of the common forms of speech whenever he conversed with Mr. Haslewood ; and, had the error been allowed to stand in the above letter, he might not have thought it extraordinary.   We think it extraordinary, as we have over and over again said, that such a man should for a single hour have been tolerated as a member of such a body.

We have now finished the ' Roxburghe Revels,' and finished the Roxburghe Club : Mr. Haslewood has finished himself.*

* The following is from the Times Newspaper :—" The publication of the late Mr. Haslewood's ' Roxburghe Revels' has recalled to our remembrance a story circulated a few years ago, relative to an erudite collector who was accustomed to boast of his discoveries in Venetian History, from the perusal of a rare 4to *De re Venatica.*   Whether this eminent Antiquarian and Linguist is at present a dead or a living ' Lion,' we cannot exactly say ; having quite forgotten his name, as well as that of his Bibliographer, who, one day, lowered his pretensions, by gravely informing him, that the Historical discoveries to which he laid claim, had been anticipated by Mr. Beckford, who, towards the close of the last century, published them to the world, under the analogous title of *Thoughts on Hunting.*   Perhaps, in default of other claimants, Mr. Haslewood's executors will administer to the anecdote.   They need not apprehend any opposition, unless it should arise from the representatives of the parties, who being employed to arrange a long-neglected Collegiate Library, placed a tract ' On Impossible Roots' among the Botanical Treatises, and enriched the class of Surgical books with *Burton's* Anatomy of Melancholy.'   We submit, that a claim might still more successfully be advanced for a learned Scotsman who not a hundred years since, in superintending the catalogue of the *law* books of a certain national library, admitted into the collection the following *legal* works :—*Acta Sanctorum,—Anthologia Græca,—The house of Peeresses, or Female Oratory.*—These entries are amusing enough, but the following is still more so :—' Joco-serius (Opizius) Dissertatio Juridica, de eo quod justum est, circa spiritus familiares fæminorum, h. e. pulices. Liberovadi, 1684 in 12mo.' !!!

APPENDIX.

I.

BIOGRAPHICAL SKETCH OF THE LATE

JOSEPH HASLEWOOD, Esq. F.S.A.*

Sept. 21. Died at Addison Road, Kensington, in his 64th year, Joseph Haslewood, Esq. of Conduit Street, Solicitor, and F.S.A.

This respectable gentleman was born in London, Nov. 5, 1769, and early in life was taken into the office of his uncle Mr. Dewberry, a solicitor in Conduit Street, whose partner aud successor in business he subsequently became.

Mr. Haslewood's fondness for early English literature and bibliography naturally led him to the collection of a considerable library of black-letter lore and Elizabethan poetry, and the pages and fly leaves of his books bear ample testimony by their numerous MS. notanda, that he was not only a collector, but a reader of the works with which his shelves were so amply furnished. In books on Angling, and in those of Hawking and field sports, his collection is confessedly unrivalled; and the productions of the private press of his friend Sir Egerton Brydges at Lee Priory, are more complete than will be probably found in the library of the worthy Baronet himself, who invariably presented a copy of every work to his friend Mr. Haslewood, who was his coadjutor also in several literary undertakings. He was

* From the Gentleman's Magazine, November 1833, page 467.

one of the founders of the Roxburghe Club, and has left a very curious manuscript volume, tracing the rise of that society, which emanated from the literati who attended the sale of the library of the late Duke of Roxburghe forming themselves into a club to commemorate the sale of the famous Boccaccio, which was purchased by the Duke of Marlborough for *two thousand two hundred and sixty pounds,* the greatest sum ever paid for a single volume, and which now forms one of the many gems in the princely library of Earl Spencer.   Mr. Haslewood's volume, under the quaint title of " Roxburghe Revels," records the annual festivities of the Club, from its first meeting at the Old St. Alban's Tavern in 1812, to the present time. In most of the notices of Mr. Haslewood which have gone the round of the daily journals, he is particularly represented as having been a *bon vivant,* to which distinction, however, Mr. Haslewood had no further claim than falls to the lot of the greater portion of mankind, in preferring a good dinner to a bad one, a sin to which, it is believed, most of the Roxburghe members are equally addicted with their late associate.   Mr. Haslewood was punctual in the discharge of his religious duties by attendance upon public worship ; and whenever ill health, or other circumstances interfered to prevent him, his constant practice was to read the church service in private.

Although neither a classical scholar nor an elegant writer, Mr. Haslewood was a laborious and faithful editor of many rare and beautiful reprints of early English poetry and prose, which might otherwise have perished ; and assisted several of the members of the Roxburghe Club in correcting and printing the volumes which they occasionally presented to the society.   The following is a list of the works in which he was connected, either as joint or sole editor, or to which he was occasional contributor :—

1807-9.   Censura Literaria.   Occasional Communications, which led to a lasting friendship with its acknowledged editor Sir Egerton Brydges.

1809.   Green-room Gossip ; or Gravity Gallinipt.   A Gallimaufry got up to guile Gymnastical and Gynecocratic Governments.   Gathered and garnished by Gridiron Gabble, Gent. Godson to Mother Goose, 1 vol. 12mo.

1809.   Battayle of Flodden Field.   Quarto, a fragment.

1810—1814. British Bibliographer. Conjointly with Sir Egerton Brydges, 4 vols. 8vo.

1810. Paradise of Dainty Devices.

1810. Tusser's Five Hundred Points of Good Husbandry. A reprint of the first edition.

1810. Italian Taylor and his Boy, of Robert Armin. Quarto.

1810. Northern Garlands. Octavo, first published anonymously by the late Joseph Ritson.

1810. Gammer Gurton's Garland. Octavo; also first published by Mr. Ritson.

1811. Arte of English Poesie, by Webster, alias George Puttenham. Quarto.

1811. Book of St. Albans, by Dame Juliana Barnes, or Berners; containing the Treatises of Hawking, Hunting, Coat-armour, Fishing, and Blasing of Arms, with a Bibliographical Introduction by Mr. Haslewood. In black letter, small folio.

1812. England's Helicon. In conjunction with Sir Egerton Brydges.

1813. Palace of Pleasure, by Robert Painter. Two volumes in quarto. Comprising some of the Tales from which Shakspeare is supposed to have drawn the subject of his dramas.

1814. Pierce the Ploughman's Crede. Quarto, in black letter, uniform with the Ploughman's Vision, edited by Dr. Whitaker.

1815. Ancient Critical Essays upon English Poets and Poesy, by Webbe, King James the First, Sir John Harrington, &c. Quarto, one volume.

1815. Mirror for Magistrates. Quarto, three volumes.

1816. Dialogues of Creatures Moralised. Quarto, black letter.

1817-18. Drunken Barnaby's Journal, seventh edition, one vol. foolscap octavo.

1819. Constable's Sonnets, 12mo.

1819. Fame's Memorial, by John Ford. Octavo, printed at Lee Priory.

1820. Drunken Barnabee's Journal. Two volumes square 12mo, uniform with the original edition, with a bibliographical introduction, proving Richard Brathwayte to have been the author.

I

1820.   Jack Jugler and Thersytes.   Two Interludes, printed from unique black letter copies, then in the possession of his friend Mr. Harding, at the private press of Lee Priory, and presented to the Members of the Roxburghe Club, at their Anniversary Meeting 1820.   Quarto.

1824.   Some Account of the Life and Writings of the late Joseph Ritson, Esq Octavo.

1827.   Wyl Bucks, his Testament, a Poem, small quarto, forty copies printed.

Mr. Haslewood was a valuable contributor to the Gentleman's Magazine, chiefly under the signature of Eu. Hood, among which may be noticed accounts of the antient theatres in London, 1813 and 1814; and a series of articles headed " Fly Leaves," commencing in 1822.

His health had been declining for several months previous to his dissolution, which occurred at Kensington, whither he had removed from Conduit Street for the benefit of his health.   Shortly prior to his decease he seemed better, so much so that his immediate relatives were engaged to dine with him on the 22d of September.   On the evening of the 21st, however, he was attacked by spasms of the heart, which terminated fatally ; and he was interred at Islington, Sept. 28.

II.

SALE OF THE LIBRARY OF THE LATE

JOSEPH HASLEWOOD, Esq. F. S. A.*

Since the publication of the Memoir of this gentleman, which appeared in the Gentleman's Magazine for November last, his memory has been assailed by a series of the bitterest and most cruel attacks that ever have been directed against a harmless individual just sunk into his grave.   His want of education, his occasional blunders arising therefrom, and his undeniably bad

* From the Gentleman's Magazine, March and June 1834, pages 286 and 606.

taste, have been blazoned to the world in the form of the severest satire, and with merciless exposure. Yet it would perhaps not be difficult to show that he has been more sinned against than sinning.

> We knew Bernardo. He was shrewd and prudent,
> Wisdom and cunning had their shares of him;
> Tho' pleas'd again with toys which children please,
> As books of fables graced with print of wood,
> Or the rare melody of some old ditty,
> That first was sung to please King Pepin's cradle.

That Mr. Haslewood was " shrewd and prudent" in professional matters, is proved by the fact, that he enjoyed, for a long series of years, a large share of business entrusted to him by the booksellers, who are themselves proverbially " shrewd and prudent" men; although it is true that, like many more eminent lawyers, he failed (as it is generally thought) in framing his own Will so to convey precisely the import of his wishes.

As a collector, also, we may term him shrewd and prudent; for by great industry in collation and careful transcription, and by the aid of his favourite binder Lewis, he converted many a fragment of little value into a book of considerable price, to the material advantage of his representatives, as the results of the recent sale have amply demonstrated.

With respect to his personal manners, he was perfectly quiet and unobtrusive in society; and therefore the gentlemen of rank and education who have composed the Roxburghe Club had no cogent reason (as his slanderer has pretended) to dismiss from their society a man possessed of very extensive information on subjects connected with their favourite pursuits. That the light in which he has placed, in his " Roxburghe Revels," the objects for which that association met at their anniversaries, is conceived in the very worst taste, we are willing to allow; but we are inclined to attribute this circumstance rather to his erroneous conception of what was humourous and witty in description, than to any actual excess in conduct. The alleged extravagance of the Roxburghe Club Dinners would equally apply, we conceive, to every party patronizing the same expensive houses; and should

rather be regarded as the tax paid for the fancied advantage of being entertained at an aristocratic tavern, with foreign cookery, and rare foreign wines
(though perhaps scarcely tasted), than as the particular profusion of the
Roxburghe Club. A retired literary student might say, and we should
agree with him, that the cost would have been far more profitably spent on
intellectual instead of sensual gratifications ; but does not this argument apply to every tavern dinner, so many of which divide the money expended,
not on the mere researches of a private literary club, but on the objects of
public charitable institutions ? And yet such dinners are considered advan-
tageous to those institutions, and promoted with that view.

But we will leave this lamentable exposure of the frailties of the dead,
with stating two or three facts, which will, we think, be taken in extenua-
tion of the reproaches cast on the reputation of our industrious and well-
intentioned friend ; and which will tend to show that, as we before hinted,
his memory has not been protected by that shield which pious relatives are
ever anxious to supply. We find that the deceased directed in his Will that
his literary property should be sold at one particular auctioneer's, but
another was selected ;* he desired it to be sold " about Easter following his
death," this wish was disregarded ; above all, and this is very important,
he required only such manuscripts should be sold as were " PROPERLY
SALEABLE," and such cautious discrimination certainly was not exercised.
There was a general outcry at the " Roxburghe Revels" being brought to
sale, and if only forty shillings had been bidden for the book, it might have
been bought in ; but as it was run up to forty pounds, that sum so far out-
weighed any scruples of respect which might have been entertained for the

---

* "—at the rooms of Mr. Sotheby, Wellington Street, Strand, being an old, eligible, fairly
conducted establishment, and certainly for many years past, and at the present period, the best
Public Mart for the sale of such kind of property." This was dated Feb. 24, 1827 ; afterwards, from a misapprehension that he had thus bequeathed a beneficiary bequest to Mr.
Sotheby, which would be liable to the legacy duty (see the whole circumstances stated at length
at the close of Messrs. Sotheby's Catalogue of Mr. Caldecott's Library), Mr. Haslewood re-
voked this direction by a codicil dated June 3, 1828, and desired a " friend " to be consulted,
" *who will probably adopt my original wish.*" In this expectation he was deceived.

character of the deceased, that the temptation could no longer be resisted. This is the palpable and barely disguised truth.

Having made these few remarks, in justice to the memory of a very old Correspondent of the Gentleman's Magazine, we proceed to give some account of the Sale. It is probably not generally known, that a large number of Mr. Haslewood's early printed books were sold by Messrs. King and Lochee in three days' sale in May 1809. The late sale, by Mr. Evans, occupied eight days in December last. Among its most prominent features was a very complete assemblage of the publications of his friend Sir Egerton Brydges; and also all the highly embellished works of Dr. Dibdin, which were sold at prices which must be very gratifying to their author. They produced, although upon small paper, upwards of L.65. The set, however, included a great many extraneous ornaments in the form of plates and privately printed tracts, among which latter the tale of " La Belle Marianne" was sold for L.1. 17s. and the " Lincoln Nosegay" for L.2. 7s. The whole series of the Roxburghe reprints, forty-four in number, was sold for L.115.; a collection of autographs, bound in three volumes, for L.61. 19s. ; and a series of more than 700 Royal Proclamations, from 1590 to 1710, in two volumes, for L.72. 9s.

A copy of the recent edition of Boswell's Johnson, by Croker, illustrated with about 50 prints, and an autograph letter of Johnson to Mr. Elphinston, L.6. 15s.

Of the works of R. Brathwait, the author (as Mr. Haslewood first ascertained) of Drunken Barnaby's Journal, he possessed a numerous list. The first edition of Barnabee's Journall was sold for L.1. 13s.; Mr. Haslewood's re-print of 1820, for L.2. 8s.; another copy, with MS. and printed additions, L.3. 10s. ; a large paper copy of his edition of 1818, illustrated with the original drawings, and unpublished prints, L. . s.; Brathwait's Golden Fleece, 1611, L.3. 5s. ; his English Gentleman and Gentlewoman, 4to, 1630-31, L.1. 7s., fol. 1641, L.1. 8s. ; his Honest Ghost, 1658, L.2. 15s. : Strappado for the Divell, 1615, L.1. 3s.; another copy, L.1. 10s.; Law of Drinking, and Smoking Age, 1617, L.2. 19s.; Nature's Embassie, 1621.

L.1. 2s.; Ragland's Niobe, on the death of Eliz. Lady Herbert, 1635 (the only perfect copy known), L.2. 19s.; Panthalia, or the Royal Romance, 1659, with a MS. key, and a note by Mr. Haslewood ascribing it to Brathwait, 10s.   With others of less variety.

	L.	s.	d.
T. Brown's Life of Haynes the Comedian, 1701, (Garrick's copy)	1	9	0
Beza's Cordial for a Sick Conscience (see British Bibl. vol. II.) .	1	0	0
Allan's Collectanea Historica de Comit. Dunelmensi (privately printed) - - - - - - - - -	7	5	0
Book of St. Alban's, edited by Mr. Haslewood in 1810, illustrated with proof prints, letters, &c. (and accompanied by an ancient hunting staff) - - - - - - - -	11	11	0
Juliana Barnes's Booke of Hawking, Huntying, and Fyshing, all three parts printed by Coplande; (the cut of the group of figures is as in Vale's edition) - - - - -	8	0	0
Sir James Boswell's Re-prints.—Churchyard's Mirror of Man, 10s.; Tractat of an Yngliss Chronicle, 16s.; Lauder's Scottish Soldier, 11s.; Buke of ye Chess, 11s.; Fig for Momus, 17s.; Lives of Sir N. Bacon, Dyer, &c. 15s.			
Buck's Eclog of Crowns and Garlands, 1605 - - -	0	13	0
Best on Hawkes and Hawking, 1619 (see Censura Literaria) -	1	4	0
Ballads.—There were about twenty quarto volumes sold in thirteen lots, to which Mr. Haslewood had given quaint alliterative titles; they averaged about a guinea a volume. Also five folio volumes of Ballads and Broadsides of the three last centuries, uniformly bound, which sold for L.17.			
Cranmer's Catechismes, the first edition, 1548 (imperfect) -	4	18	0
Charton's Life of Dean Nowell, 1809, illustrated with prints, and three documents relative to a controversy between Nowell and Sir E. Hoby - - - - - - -	5	15	6
Churton's Lives of Bishop Smyth and Sir R. Sutton (illustrated)	2	16	0
Chattertoniana; a collection of Chatterton's works and the publications respecting him, uniformly bound in 16 vols. 8vo. and one quarto, in the latter of which, among several letters, were			

autographs of Chatterton, offering the tragedy of Ella to Dods-
ley, and soliciting the advance of a guinea - - 18 0 0
Drummond of Hawthornden's Poems, 1656 - - 3 1 0
Caveat for Christmas, or a short discourse of Sport, Play, or Re-
creation in general, by N. T. C. 1622, a manuscript, and a MS.
Sermon at Paul's Cross, Nov. 15, 1621. - - 1 12 0
Churchyardes Choise, in Prose and Verse, 1579 - - 1 18 0
Collection of Odes by Poets Laureat, and Parodies on them, variations of God Save the King, Rule Brittania, &c. 4to. - 2 2 0
Collectanea; Extracts from Newspapers, Reviews, &c. 4to. 3 15 0
Cambridge.—Worke for Cutlers, acted in a Show at Cambridge,
1615; Merrie Dialogue between Band, Cuffe, and Ruffe, as performed at Cambridge, *interleaved with MS. variations* " as per-
formed at Oxford," 1615; Exchange Ware, as acted at Cam-
bridge, 1615, a MS. copy of verses spoken by Dulman (a character in Ignoramus) and John a Styles - - 6 6 0
Catalogue Raisonne of the select collection of Engravings of an
Amateur (T. Wilson, Esq.) privately printed, 1828 - 2 17 0
Dialogue of Creatures Moralised, edited by Haslewood, and printed on one side of the paper only, for the purpose of being more
fully illustrated with prints - - - - 5 18 0
Donne's Poems, in MS. (but only one not in printed Works) 1 16 0
England's Helicon, by Brydges, 1812, with some Songs, &c. of
which only a few copies were printed - - - 1 10 0
Fly Leaves, the series of articles by Mr. Haslewood which ap-
peared in the Gentleman's Magazine, with additional notes 1 11 0
Treatise on Fishing with an Angle, a MS. of the early part of the
15th century (see Haslewood's Account of the Book of St.
Alban's, p. 63) - - - - - 3 0 0
Davenant's Gondibert, 1651. Certain Verses on Gondibert (in
ridicule of it), 1653. Gondibert Vindicated, 1655 (very rare) 0 18 0
Daniel's Panegyrike of James I. and Defence of Ryme, 1603 0 17 0
Collection of Epitaphs, 2 vols. 1806, large paper, with additions, 2 10 0

Fitz-Geffry's Elegies, Satyres, and Epigrams, 1620 (part MS.)	0	15	0
The Fisher's Garland, 11 vols. 1821–1831, *Newcastle* -	1	6	0
The Art of Angling, a MS. about 1618, as supposed by Mr. H.	2	13	0
Nobbes compleat Troller, 1682, 8vo. the original edition, with some MS. notes by W. White, of Crickhowell - -	1	2	0
The same edition in 4to. with the same additions - -	1	11	6
Collectanea Grayiana, being Gray's Poems, by Wakefield, and Poems and Letters, by Mason, illustrated by a copious collection of fragments - - - - -	2	12	6
Gilbert's Young Angler's Delight, no date, (only known copy)	2	12	6
Ellis's Catalogue of Books on Angling, privately printed, 1811, with numerous additions by Mr. Haslewood - - -	2	2	0
Fowldes's Strange, Wonderful, and Bloudy Battell between Frogs and Mice, paraphrastically done into English Heroycal Verse, 1603 - - - - - - - - -	3	12	0
Green's History of Frier Bacon and Frier Bungay - -	2	2	0
The Noble Art of Venerie, or Hunting, 1573, part MS. and illustrated (attributed to Gascoigne) - - - - -	2	2	0
The Noble Art of Venerie, with the Measures of Blowing, 1611	1	13	0
Sir J. Harington's Epigrams and Poems. The author's autograph MS. containing some unpublished pieces and variations from printed works - - - - - - - -	20	10	0
Holland's Buke of the Howlat (by Laing, for Bannatyne Club, 1823) - - - - - - -	2	2	0
Heywood's Works, 1598 - - - - -	2	4	0
Howard's Miraculous Life and Death of St. Marie of Ægipt, a poem, supposed to be printed at Douay about 1685-8 -	1	5	0
Cronycles of Englande (St. Alban's) Wynkyn de Worde, 1520 -	2	18	0
Home's Dramatic Works, 1760 (presentation copy to Lady Harvey)	1	0	0
Junius,—a Collection of the Essays on the author, by Coventry, G. Chalmers, Taylor, Duppa, Girdlestone, Blakeway, &c. 3 vols.	1	19	0
Institution of a Gentleman. Imprinted by Marshe, 1568 -	2	5	0
Lyrical Gleanings, comprising Madrigals, Odes, Songs, and Son-			

nets, chiefly by anonymous writers of the 16th and 17th centuries (once intended for publication, and a prospectus issued by Mr. Triphook*)   -   -   -   -   -   2   3   0

Easton on Human Longevity, 1792, interleaved, in two vols. with numerous additions   -   -   -   -   -   1   3   0

Merry Musician, with the Music, 2 vols. 1730   -   -   1   12   0

Kemp's Nine Daies Wonder, performed in a Daunce from London to Norwich, MS. the only printed copy being in the Bodl. Lib.   1   14   0

Another transcript of the same, formerly the Duke of Roxburghe's   1   17   0

Leigh's Accedence of Armorie, 1568   -   -   -   1   4   0

Livre de Roy Modus et de la Royne Racio, qui parle de la Chasse a toutes bestes sauvages et de Faulconnerie, (cuts) *Paris*, 1526   1   10   0

Loniceri Venatus et Aucupium (many cuts) *Franc.* 1582   -   1   1   0

Hawking and Hunting. Prints and Persian Drawings, and eight pieces by Dietrich Mayer, 1599, bound in a folio volume   6   16   6

Octavian, a Romance, by Conybeare; privately printed, *Oxf.* 1809   0   17   0

The Birth, Death, and Resurrection of our Saviour; written in the first person. A Dialogue between St. Bernard and the Virgin Mary, a MS. on vellum, with a transcript and glossorial index   -   -   -   -   -   -   4   4   0

Parker's Nightingale, 1632, privately reprinted by A. Strettell, esq.   0   7   0

Pope.—Tracts on the life and poetical character of Pope, by Lord Byron, Bowles, Gilchrist, Roscoe, D'Israeli, Campbell, &c. &c. 2 vols.   -   -   -   -   -   -   -   3   13   6

State Poems, including the Worms, a Satire by Pope; the original broadside, and MS. notes by Mr. Haslewood   -   1   11   6

Poetical Biography, in 13 vols. consisting of the Lives by Winstanly, Langbaine, Gildon, Jacob, Whincop. Egerton's Theatrical Remembrancer; the Prompter by Mr. Haslewood, and a very extensive miscellaneous collection of materials, *with a manuscript index*   -   -   -   -   -   -   23   0   0

A collection of Penny Histories in 6 volumes   -   -   6   10   0

Another collection, in five volumes   -   -   -   4   4   0

K

Printing.—Willett on the origin of Printing, *Newc.* 1820. Sant-
ander on the same, 1819. Hodgson on Stereotype Printing,
1820, and Hodgson's Memoirs of Ged, 1820. All large paper,
of which there are only 36 copies of the third, and 30 of the
others - - - - - - 1 7 0
Pursuits of Literature, both editions; Burdon's Remarks on the
same; other tracts by Mr. Mathias; the Irish Pursuits of Literature, &c. 4 vols. - - - - 3 3 0
Psalms of David, translated into four languages, by Slayter, 1643,
with music, one piece of which has the name of J. Milton, supposed to be the father of the poet - - - 2 5 0
Ritson's Robin Hood, 2 vols. 1795, and an additional volume of
Collections on the same subject - - - - 11 15 0
Ritson's Bibliographia Poetica, 1802, with copious notes, made
with a view to a new edition - - - 3 3 0
Another copy with MS. notes by Mr. Park, and a letter of Ritson 1 9 0
A third copy, interleaved with MS. notes by Malone - 1 1 0
Haslewood's Life of Ritson, 1824, the only copy on large paper,
and a printed Catalogue of Ritson's Library 1 10 0
A curious volume of Ritsoniana, 1824, printed and MS. - 6 6 0
Rich's Mirrour of Mercy in the midst of Misery (verse) 1654 0 15 0
Maxwell's Albion's Remembrance of Fred. Count Palatine and
Elizabeth, 1613 - - - - - 1 0 0
Nash's Summer's Last Will, a Pleasant Comedie, 1600 - 2 0 0
Fyne's Moryson's Itinerary, containing his Ten Years' Travels,
1617 - - - - - - 6 0 0
Rump Poems and Songs, both parts, 1662 - - - 2 2 0
Ramsay's New Miscellany of Scots Songs, 1727 (presumed 2d edit.) 1 7 0
Shakspeariana, two sets of tracts each in 12 volumes, each 8 8 0
Shakspeariana, a volume of cuttings from books and newspapers 2 11 0
Ireland's Shakespeare Forgery, eight volumes of tracts on - 6 10 0
Shenstone's Poems. *Oxford,* 1737. First edit. which was sup-
pressed - - - - - - 3 1 0

Sale Catalogues, an extraordinary quantity of, in 98 volumes   7   0   0

Roxburghe Club Books, a complete collection, in number 44, [said to be purchased for the Duke of Buccleuch]   -   -   115   0   0

A Roxburghe Garland, by J. Boswell, 1817   -   -   1   11   6

Roxburghe Revels, a journal by Mr. Haslewood of the Proceedings of the Roxburghe Club, and the foundation of the attack noticed in our introductory remarks.   40   0   0

MANUSCRIPTS.

Autographs, a valuable collection, in three volumes*   -   61   19   0

Upton de Studio Militari, MS. of 15th century, partly on vellum   2   3   0

A fragment of Chaucer's Canterbury Tales   -   -   -   8   8   0

The Compendion Historiall, translated in manner of pastyme, by Thomas Wall, Windsor Herald, 1538, containing autographs of Jane Wryothesley, Countess of Southampton, and Thos. Treachory, Somerset Herald   -   -   -   -   -   3   1   0

William Percy's Comedies, Pastorals, and Epigrams; the MS. from which Mr. Lloyd printed two plays for the Roxburghe Club in 1824   -   -   -   -   -   -   -   12   12   0

Destruction of Jerusalem; vellum MS. 14th century   -   -   12   12   0

The original Register of the Performances at Covent Garden Theatre from 1750 to 1773, by C. M. Rich   -   -   3   5   0

Chaucer's Legend of Good Women, a MS. on paper   -   7   0   0

A volume of original Contracts between Authors and Publishers   4   0   0

A collection of MSS. relating to the Fastolfe family   -   13   0   0

Stimulus Conscientiæ, by Roll, a vellum MS. 14th century   8   5   0

---

*Among them was the original Signature Paper of the Members of the Middlesex Association, 1745, containing most of the Nobility of the day; and Lord Strafford's last Letter to his Son, dated from the Tower, 11th May 1641, the day before his execution, a beautiful specimen of his parental affection and magnanimity: " Be sure to avoyd as much as you can to enquire after those y^t have been sharp in the jugement toward me : And I charge you never to suffer thought of revenge to enter into your hart."

Portsmouth Theatre account-book, 1771-1774　-　-　-　5　7　6
Papers relating to the office of Revels, 16th and 17th century　9　15　0
Wickliffe's New Testament, a fine vellum manuscript, 14th century 43　0　0
A common-place book of Poetry, collected by Richard Jackson,1623 10　15　0
Mr. Haslewood's correspondence with his literary friends relative
　　to Richard Braithwait, and an autograph of the latter　-　4　4　0
Psalms by Sir Philip Sidney and Mary Countess of Pembroke,
　　differing from the printed copy ; a MS. formerly belonging to
　　the Harringtons.　　　　　　　　　　　　　　　2　9　0

———

Paradise of Dainty Devises, 4to, 1585　　　-　　-　4　10　0
Tracts on the Drama, 28 vols. 8vo, and one 4to　-　-　24　10　0
Green Room Gossip, by Mr. Haslewood, 1809, prepared for a new
　　edition　-　-　-　-　-　-　2　7　0
Watson Taylor's Poems and Plays (privately printed) 1830　0　13　0
Watson Taylor's Profligate, a Comedy (privately printed) 1820　1　12　0
Walton's Complete Angler, first edition, 1653, L.13. 5s. ; second edition,
　　1655, L.5. 5s ; third edition, 1661, L.3. 6s. ; the same with new title,
　　1664, L.3. 6s. ; fourth edition, 1668, L.3. 1s. ; fifth edition, 1676, L.3.
　　15s. ; sixth edition, 1750, L.2. 2s. ; first edition by Hawkins, 1760, L.3.
　　3s. ; second edition, 1766, L.1. 11s. 6d. ; Bagster's edit. 1808, illustrated,
　　L.5. 7s. 6d. his second edition, 1813, illustrated, L.4. ; another copy, illus-
　　trated, and including the portrait of Walton by Bovi, L.5. 10s.
Walton's Lives, 1670, with autograph inscription to Beacham　2　4　0
His Life of Bp. Sanderson, 1678, with corrections by his own hand 0　19　0
Watson's Collection of Scots Poems, 3 parts, 1706-13, Ritson's copy 2　13　0
Plays, Players, and Playhouses ; a collection by Mr. Haslewood,
　　in nine quarto volumes, principally relating to the London
　　theatres　-　-　-　-　-　20　0　0
Robinson's Rewards of Wickedness, 1574 (poetry)　-　2　10　0
Ritson's Bibliographia Poetica, interleaved and enlarged　-　4　4　0
Spenser's Faerie Queene, 1st. edit. 2 vols 1790-96.　-　-　3　5　0

III.

OBSERVATIONS ON THE ATTACK ON THE LATE

JOSEPH HASLEWOOD, Esq. F.S.A.

BY THE REV. DR. T. F. DIBDIN.

LEST " *silence* " should be construed into impotence, or an inability to meet the charges, direct or implied, which are contained in four successive articles upon the late Mr. HASLEWOOD and the ROXBURGHE CLUB, written in the Athenæum of January 1834—and in which articles the characters of others, as well as of my own, may be supposed to be more or less impugned—I will take leave to submit a few remarks in the shape of a REPLY to the articles in question. But, first, I beg to say a few words upon the transaction itself, which *led* to the communications in the Athenæum. I agree with the writer of those articles in thinking that such a MS. volume as that entitled the ROXBURGHE REVELS should never have seen the pnblic light. As there was nothing to call for—so there was nothing to justify—such an exposure. Mr. Haslewood died a bachelor, in comparatively easy circumstances. The whole produce of his library, whatever that might be, was to go, unburdened, to his heirs, relations, or legatees. He had often told me, in the earlier part of our acquaintance, that he would refuse a *thousand guinea cheque* for his books. They produced at his death about L.2,500; the WHOLE being so much more than any person or persons could reasonably expect for *themselves,* as their owner might have sold his books in his lifetime, and put the amount of the sale into his pocket, without there being the shadow of a *right* to call him to an account for such a proceeding. This point is, I think, as clear as the sun at noon-day.

However, it is too well known that Mr. Haslewood did *not* do so ; but dying, he left two executors—one of whom, who was his brother, declined to act. The acting executor, an old and intimate friend of the deceased, resolved to show his *affectionate respect* for his memory, by *selling* this volume with the whole of the library. There is no accounting for tastes : and one has heard of being " defended from friends, and taking care of one's self against enemies." Poor Haslewood was in no condition to do the latter ; and, accordingly, THIS VOLUME—the concoction of one in his gayer and unsuspecting moments—the repository of private, confidential communications —a mere memorandum-book of what had passed at convivial meetings, and in which " winged words" and flying notes of many gentlemen and friends were *obviously* incorporated—this volume it was resolved TO SELL. Something like an unctuous balm to something like a misgiving conscience was also resolved, in the first place, to be administered, by *putting in* the book at such a price as it was supposed would beat down all opposition ; and I have reason to believe that TWENTY GUINEAS was the sum in contemplation. The mode adopted to accomplish that end was singular enough. It was as if pouring oil into a fire should extinguish the flames.

Long before the sale, the book became almost public property. It was allowed to travel eastwardly and westwardly. Not only was the substance of the greater part of its " C. Mery tales " noised abroad, but it became stripped of portions of its contents. Never did spoliation assume a more praiseworthy character. Never was an act of robbery more to be commended. The only subject of lamentation is, that it did not go FURTHER. If the executor, in the just exercise of what he thought to be a discretionary power, suffered A, B, C, to receive back *their* contributions, why, I ask, did he not extend the exercise of that power to D ? If the genuineness of the *entirety* of the volume be invaded, upon what principle is the trespasser to *stop*? Of ALL the contributors to that unparalleled *olla podrida*, I think that the writer of these pages had as great a right as any one to receive back his *own*. Above all, should I have desired the letter of Sir Walter Scott— which was given to the deceased as a document *per se*, and not for his family to enjoy its *proceeds*. As to the letter of Lord Althorp to me, and my note to the deceased, which have served the purpose of indiscreet, if not indecent remark, it was, perhaps, not to be expected that an executor, so wholly absorbed in doing JUSTICE to the memory of his departed friend, should think of restoring either. The volume was bought at the sale by Mr. Thorpe for L.40, and by him offered, through me, to the purchase of the Roxburghe Club. Of course, no gentleman would think of putting his hand into his pocket with a view, as it might have been said, of hushing up any strictures advanced upon SUCH an association. The characters and rank in life of the members placed them far above it.

In consequence, the ROXBURGHE REVELS became the property of one who " resolved to purchase it at any price, that he might gratify curiosity- and give the readers [of the Athenæum] its principal contents." And further, he " hoped and believed he should execute his task without giving offence in any quarter." The *proof* of this friendliness of disposition is remarkably verified in his fourth and last communication, when he hopes to be able " to give the Roxburghe Club its COUP DE GRACE ;" and that he " shall be happy to have done *with*, as well as done *for*, both Mr. Haslewood and the Club." To be sure, there is no " giving offence " to people when they are DEAD. Again, in the same communication :—" the Club is *extinct*, and Haslewood has *extinguished* it." A little further : " the anniversary dinner of 1833 is the *last* it will ever celebrate." And the concluding sentence runs thus :—" We have now finished the Roxburghe Revels and finished the Roxburghe Club. Mr. Haslewood has finished himself." I place these points in front of this reply, to shew the *quo animo* of the writer ; and how very strange and startling it is, to see a man going about with a drawn sword or bludgeon in his hand, in order to transfix or knock down individuals as he meets them, by way of gratifying curiosity, and " not giving offence in any quarter."

Renewing the expression of my entire accordance with this writer in the unpardonably bad taste—to give it no *harsher* name—which could have sanctioned the sale of the " Roxburghe Revels," I must be allowed to ask the censurer of such a measure, upon what plea or principle HE could have contributed to give *a more extensive publicity* to the contents of the volume in question ? To have been instrumental to the gibes and jeers of a sale-room, were sufficiently indefensible ; but, with this *conviction* of the gross impropriety of *such* conduct in the writer's mind, to have *deliberately* spread

far and wide, by means of an ably-conducted hebdomadal journal, the whim-
sicalities and harmless absurdities of the book now under consideration, is
utterly irreconcileable to reason and honest dealing. It is quite evident from
the beginning, that the anonymous writer was determined upon the measure
of exposure : he was resolved to have the book, *coute qu'il coute*—and gave
the purchaser at the sale five guineas for his bargain. He seems to have
rushed forward as a vulture upon his prey. The dead body of poor Haslewood is mangled with his talons—and yet all this is undertaken, as he com-
placently tells us, " to gratify curiosity," and with the hope of being " able
to execute his task without giving offence to any one." If the deceased had
been the weak, harmless, ignorant, and puzzle-headed creature described by
this anonymous libeller, why take so much pains to

> " . . . . draw his frailties from their drear abode ?"

And why, on *dramatic* points, betray such unusual sensitiveness and acri-
mony of feeling and expression ? There seems throughout the whole to be
something like an under current of rivalry in the *histrionic* department.

To descend to a few particulars. The spirit or *principle* of this attack
upon the memory of my departed friend, is to me sufficiently revolting. To
kick a man when he is *down*—to kick him when he is lying upon his back
IN HIS COFFIN—is so thoroughly unenglishman and unchristianlike, that I
have no words to express my mingled contempt and abhorrence of such a
proceeding. Mr. Haslewood is no sooner at rest in his grave, than this
writer tells us *who* and *what* he was :—where and how he was *born*. What
does it matter " *where* and *how* " a man is BORN ?

> " Honour and Shame from no *condition* rise :
>   ACT WELL YOUR PART—*there* all the honour lies."

In what sort of homes were Shakspeare, and Milton, and Newton born ? To
be sure, my friend must not be mentioned in the same sentence with these
illustrious names : but the principle or *position* is confirmed by such an illus-

tration. Horace tells Mæcenas, that when he comes to pay him a visit, he must not expect to find " ivory ornaments or a gilded ceiling under his roof:" nor anything but (what might be translated into) the *vin ordinaire*, or *vin du pays*, when he comes to dine with him.* When I call to mind what I have heard, and *believe*, of the early manhood of the deceased, the wonder may be that he lived to the protracted period of his life (sixty-four years,) and was allowed, through a merciful Providence, to attain the little comfort and comparative distinction which latterly awaited him. Is a man to be pointed at, or hooted at, because, late in life, he has associated with gentlemen—when his evil stars, at an earlier period, had driven him in an opposite direction ? Throughout the whole of this writer's strictures, he boldly affirms, although necessarily he was never present, that the Members of the Roxburghe Club were shocked and disgusted with the conversation of the deceased. The assertion is CONTRARY TO TRUTH. Never was speech more harmless than that which fell from his lips. As above observed, it was only *Haslewoodian*.

As to the allusions to, or express mention made of, myself, I desire not to receive the standard of good breeding at the hands of this writer. In other respects, he may as well be informed that I am not the Secretary—that I receive no emolument—that the office of Vice-President is one of no trouble and of no indignity : further, that I have no Journal, or RIVAL book of REVELS, to bequeath for the benefit of such as, like himself, " hope to give no offence" by trampling upon the dead, and indirectly traducing the living. So short-sighted were this writer's views, or rather so consummate his vanity, and audacious his prediction of the extinction of the Roxburghe Club in consequence of *his* anathemas, that, on the vacancies occasioned by the deaths of Mr. Haslewood and Mr. Heber, and after the Athenæum articles

---

* " Non ebur, neque aureum
    Mea renidet in domo lacunar."
                Lib. ii. Ode 18.
  " Vile potabis modicis Sabinum
    Cantharis."   Lib. i. Ode 20.

L

had appeared, our venerable President, although in indifferent health, came to town expressly to fill those vacancies : when the elections of Mr. ARCH-DEACON BUTLER and Sir STEPHEN GLYNN, Bart. M.P., gave no signs of *morbidity* in any portion of the body corporate of ROXBURGHERS ! So much for a little too much confidence in the exercise of unrestrained scurrility.

It is necessary to correct a few ERRORS in this memorable attack. I wish I could call them, in the language of Quintilian, " *dulcia vitia.*" On the death of Mr. Dodd, it is said that application was made to " Mr. Bliss, son of a bookseller at Oxford," to become his successor. Application *was* made to Mr. Bliss ; and I felt as anxious as my departed friend for his election :— for his talents (evinced by his edition of Wood's *Athenæ Oxonienses*) would have done credit to the choice. But the application was made to the Rev. Philip Bliss, of St. John's College, and now Dr. Bliss, Registrar of the University of Oxford. The father of Dr. Bliss was a *clergyman*, and not a *bookseller*. But what if he *had* been ? The late Rev. Peter Elmsly, Principal of St. Alban's Hall, was the nephew of a bookseller of that name in the Strand : and when did Oxford boast a more perfect ATTIC-GREEK SCHOLAR than that excellent man ? The writer further says, that application was made by Mr. Haslewood on the death of Sir Mark Sykes, for the admission of an individual into the Club, whom he chooses to designate as a sort of literary *Paul Pry*—and whose admission, he implies, would have disgraced it. I can only say, that, leaving the individual here *knooted*, to fight his own battle, which I presume him to be capable of doing, I do not *believe* the statement. It was most likely to have come to my knowledge ; but it did *not*. The amount of the contribution to raise a monument to the memory of Caxton, is so loosely stated by him, that one would think it was only L.2. 2s. The members *never* objected, for one moment, to advance this sum per head, with equal readiness, as their quotas for the anniversary dinners. What they *did* object to, was *this* :—to contribute towards the payment of L.120 for the *fees* of erection of the monument. As above intimated, the parochial officers of St. Margaret, much to their honour, allowed this *Roxburghian* tribute of respect to the memory of our first English printer to be placed upon the walls of the church, or rather over the vestry-door, in the vestibule, as you ascend the staircase, FREE OF ALL CHARGES : forming, in this instance, a striking and honourable contrast to their neighbours.

It is time to make an end. In what has been here advanced, I have had neither selfish nor sinister views to gratify. There is a *dead* as well as a living reputation both to defend and to substantiate ; and I trust that I have effected this for my departed friend. In so doing I have not held him up as the mirror of literary or antiquarian knighthood. Far from it : but there is a difference between the charge of almost drivelling idiocy and an uneducated understanding ; especially, too, as in this instance, the former seems to be accompanied with an imputation of disgusting vulgarity. As to the factitious titles attached by my friend to certain volumes of minor poetry, such as " *Garlands of Gravity—Eleemosynary Emporium—Noddy's Nuncheon—Poverty's Pot-Pourri—Mumper's Medley—Nutmegs for Nightingales,*" &c. which brings down the terrible wrath of the critic, I see nothing so formidably repulsive in these titles. A man has surely a right to call his books, as to call his dogs, by what titles and names he pleases ; and we should no more quarrel with Mr. Haslewood for the former, than we should for having called one dog *Pincher,* another *Boxer,* and a third *Blucher :* with this difference, that Blucher was at times a very troublesome, if not dangerous, animal ; whereas " Nutmegs for Nightingales " might have continued harmless, as well as untasted and untouched, upon the shelf for centuries. Mr. Evans has well and sensibly designated the " Roxburghe Revels," as " a very curious and whimsical record." It is nothing more.

I admit, freely admit, that my friend's style was, in short, *sui generis ;* delectably original ; and at times irresistibly laughter-provoking. Yet he often seemed to be " near a good thing." He went " about it and about it," and was within " an ace " of its discovery. Then, all at once, he would strike off in a wild and unsearchable path. But enough. The deceased was capable of something like " good stuff :" and had he been allowed to concentrate his COLLECTIONS with a view to a new edition of *Warton's History of English Poetry,* with its enlargement to the present time—and of which it was in contemplation, some dozen years ago, to propose the *Editorship* to Mr. SOUTHEY—we had received an invaluable acquisition to our national literature.   Moreover, had Mr. *Haslewood* found encouragement to give us a new edition of *Ritson's Bibliographia Poetica* (to which his additions were very considerable), and which I believe he would have done with a very slender remuneration, we should have sincerely thanked him for his toil, and considered him in any light but that " of a driveller or a dolt."*

* The supposed dissolution of the Roxburghe Club has been again recently asserted, as will be seen from the following extract from the Standard :—

Thursday, November 10, 1836.—" The once popular Roxburghe Book Club seems rapidly approaching towards a dissolution. The last anniversary held at the Clarendon—by the absence of many of the most convivial and ardent members, among whom were the Dukes of Devonshire and Sutherland, Earl Spencer, and Lord Morpeth,—evinced evident signs of consummation."   This bold assertion produced the following answer :—

To the Editor of the Standard.

November 12, 1836.

Sir,—You are generally well advised on all subjects, but the paragraph which has lately appeared in your paper respecting the Roxburghe Club, shows how many mistakes may be compressed into six lines. So far from " approaching towards a dissolution," the Club was never in so prosperous a state as at the present moment, owing to the zeal and judgment which have been evinced by its noble President [Lord Viscount Clive]. At the last meeting, so despondingly alluded to in your paper, five additional members were elected, and many valuable regulations for the future government of the Club were unanimously adopted.

The " conviviality" of the Duke of Devonshire, Earl Spencer, and Lord Morpeth,† is, indeed, high matter upon which we will not enter, never having had the pleasure of witnessing it ; but where did the writer draw his information, when he speaks of the ardour of the present Earl Spencer as a book-collector.?

Amongst the absentees enumerated by your correspondent, are the Duke of Sutherland and Lord Morpeth.   Now the Duke of S. was not absent.   Lord Morpeth was ; but this may be satisfactorily accounted for, as his Lordship is not a member of the Club.   Your's,

BLACK LETTER.

† Although his Lordship has the countenance of the celebrated Liston, it is not understood that he possesses any of his humour.

IV.

ACCOUNT OF THE OLD LONDON THEATRES,

BY THE LATE

JOSEPH HASLEWOOD, Esq. F. S. A.*

Mr. URBAN. *August 5, 1813.*

There can be few readers of our antient Dramatic Pieces, but must have experienced some difficulty in ascertaining at what Theatre the representations were made, where the title-pages express the play to have been acted by the servants of " his" or " her Majesty ;" or those of the " Prince" or " the Lord Admiral," &c. &c. ; and in an attempt to throw some light upon the subject, by a very considerable enlargement of the *Notitia Dramatica,* published by the late Mr. Egerton, I have been led to form distinct articles of each theatre. Brief as those articles may appear, and little more than " brick and mortar history," I cannot help believing they derive from the subject, sufficient interest to obtain a place in your columns, which I am induced to request, from a hope that general perusal may lead to discussion and information, with a correction of any misstatement of mine, before they are collected in a volume upon the subject of the English Drama, which has been some time preparing for publication.

---

* As the reader has heard so much on both sides relative to Mr. Haslewood's literary qualifications, he will not, probably, be displeased to have the means afforded him of judging for himself; with this view the following very curious, and amusing papers, by that gentleman, on the Ancient Theatres of London, have been reprinted from the Gentleman's Magazine.

That such an attempt, particularly while treating of the earlier theatres, must derive considerable advantage from Mr. Malone's *History of the Stage,* cannot be doubted, and a general acknowledgment may suffice at present ; at the same time, the reading of the " black letter " tracts, to know what our ancestors read, now so prevalent, cannot leave a doubt that many passages may yet be gathered from those works, which will serve to elucidate the customs of the stage, and throw considerable light on the infancy of the Drama.

Convinced of the imperfections of my own attempt, I am anxious to seek the liberal assistance of others, and look with confidence to the information and suggestions of your Correspondents, whether communicated through the medium of your pages, or confided to your worthy printer, for

Your's, &c.   Eu. Hood.

THE FORTUNE THEATRE.—This Theatre stood between Golden-lane and White-cross Street. By a contract, dated January 8, 1599, which Mr. Malone has printed at length in the History of the Stage, Henslowe and Alleyn, the actors, agreed with Peter Street a carpenter, for the " erectinge, buildinge, and setting up of a new house and stage for a play-house" at this place ; and as the intended building was not specified by any name in the contract, it becomes probable this must have been the first theatre built on that spot. The cost of erecting was L.520. By the contract, it was to consist of three stories in height, containing " fower convenient divisions for gentlemen's roomes, and other sufficient and convenient divisions for twopennie roomes, with necessarie seates to be placed and sett as well in those roomes as throughout all the rest of the galleries of the said howse," and to have " divisions without and within." The " gentlemen's roomes" were the boxes, and by that title they were repeatedly mentioned as early as 1609.* Twopenny rooms might be the part which was until lately

* " 'Tis euen as common to see a bason at the Church doore as a box at a Play-house." *Every Woman in her Humour,* 1609. Again in Decker's Gull's Hornbook, 1609.

called slips ; and the area or yard, now forming the pit, seems to have been entirely open, and filled promiscuously by the crowd.*

The Fortune was opened by Allen, with the Lord Admiral's servants,† who had previously performed at the Rose, and who, in 1603, changed their patron for the gallant Henry Frederick, Prince of Wales. It has been described as a " vast theatre," and certainly continued a favourite with the public for several years. In Albumazar, performed at Cambridge, in 1614, Trinculo says, " I will confound her with compliments drawn from the plays I see at the *Fortune* and *Red Bull,* where I learn all the words I speak and understand not." And John Melton, in his Astrologaster or the Figvre Caster, 1620, [small 4to, p. 31,] describes the representation of the *History of Dr. Faustus,*‡ at this theatre, as follows : " Another (he says) will foretel of lightning and thunder that shall happen such a day, when there are no such inflamations seene, except a man goe to the Fortune in Golding-lane, to see the tragedie of Doctor Faustus. There indeede a man may behold shagge-hayr'd deuills runne roaring ouer the stage with squibs in their mouthes, while drummers make thunder in the tyring-house, and the twelue-penny hirelings make artificiall lightnings in their heauens."||

* In the Play of *Nobody and Somebody,* 1601, it is said,

"Somebody once pickt a pocket in this play-house yard,
Was hoysted on the Stage and sham'd about it."

And another trait of this portion of the auditory, occurs in the prologue to the " *Hog has lost his Pearl,* acted by the London Prentices :

"We are not halfe so skil'd as strowling players,
Who could not please here as at country fairs ;
We may be pelted off, for ought we know,
With apples, eggs, or stones from thence *below ;*
In which weele craue your friendship, if we may,
And you shall haue a dance worth all the play."

† The Lord Admiral Nottingham.

‡ This was one of the most popular productions of Christopher Marlow. Eight 4to editions are known : viz. 1604, 1611, 1616, 1619, 1624, 1631, 1661, and 1663.

|| The noise of fireworks, and letting off chambers, or the clamour of fighting, was then introduced into almost every theatrical representation ; and although not incidental to the piece,

This Theatre took fire at 12 at night on December 9, 1621, and was entirely destroyed.   However, being popular, and the concern neither over-
burdened with the incumbrances attached to modern theatres, or the undertaking enfeebled by a divided proprietorship, it was speedily rebuilt, on
an extended scale, forming " a large, round, brick building," with the figure
of Fortune in the front, as described in Heywood's *English Traveller*,
1633 :

> —— " A Statue in the fore-front of your house
> For euer ; like the picture of Dame Fortune
> Before the Fortune play-house."

The new theatre was opened by the Palsgrave's servants, who appear to
have continued performing there until 1640, when they removed to the Red
Bull.   That company was succeeded by the Prince's, which contrived to act
occasionally, nowithstanding the order made by Parliament, in July 1647,
for the suppressing of Plays and Play-houses ; nor did they finally desist
until the peremptory ordinance of February 13, 1647-8, for the dismantling
of Play-houses was issued.   Amidst these contending difficulties, the rent of
the Theatre falling in arrear, the Trustees of Dulwich College (to which
charity the Playhouse had been devised by the will of Allen) took possession on the 21st of November, 1649 ; and upon the Archbishop's visitation

---

the custom was often preserved after a more vulgar manner, by attaching crackers to the slops
of the clown.   The system fell into disuse about 1620.   In the prologue to the *Two Merry
Milk Maids*, printed in that year, the omission is accounted for as " the stage being reformed ;"
and the Author prays " for your owne good, *you in the yard*," will lend ears, in order to well
understand and relate on returning home

> —————————" 'tis a fine play,
> For we have in't a coniurer, a deuill,
> And a clown too :—But I fear the euill,
> In which, perhaps, vnwisely we may faill,
> Of wanting squibs and crackers at their tail."

in 1667, it was stated that the College " had been brought in debt considerably by the *fall* of the Fortune Play-house."*

In February 1661, the site and ground adjoining were publicly advertised to be let for building upon, and that " twenty-three tenements might be erected with gardens ;" but the proposal did not succeed, as appears by the above representation to the Archbishop of the impoverishment of the College by the *falling in* of the tenantcy.

This theatre is mentioned on several occasions in the Public Journals under the title of the " Old Play-House in Red-cross Street ;" and being used for a secret conventicle, was visited by the Officers of Justice, in the attempt to suppress those meetings, as late as November 1682.†

WHITEFRIARS THEATRE.—The scite of this Theatre lay between the Eastern gates of the Temple and Water-lane, Fleet Street. It is enumerated by a Writer, in 1628, for one of those pulled down by the cautious citizens soon after the year 1580 ; to which Mr. Malone adds, " the theatre in Blackfriars not being within the liberties of the City of London, escaped the fury of these fanaticks.‡ Probably there is some mistake in this representation, as the line of the ancient wall of the City, as described in the old maps, appears more likely to have enclosed the ground-plot of Blackfriars than Whitefriars ; and the theatre of the latter certainly stood upon the precincts of the once-noted " kingdom of Alsatia," whose lawless origin is not ascertained, but where neither the civic magistrate, nor other legal officer, ventured to appear until near the close of the seventeenth century.||

* Lysons's Environs, vol. I. p. 104.

† It then had avenues to both Red-cross Street and White-cross Street ; a circumstance that, in several instances, enabled the preachers to escape from their pursuers.—A View of the Theatre is inserted in the Londinia Illustrata, No. 11.

‡ Reed's Shakspeare, vol III. p 46-7.

|| About May 1697, some of the public journals relate that the bailiffs, by combining in a body, had then first overcome the difficulty of making an arrest in the White-friars ; and which having been repeated in two or three instances, several persons that resided there as a privileged place, removed to the Mint, Southwark, then equally lawless, for better security of their persons ; and which circumstance, probably, first occasioned the disbanding the once-renowned order of the Squires of Alsatia.

So few and indistinct are the traces of this theatre, that the period of it being rebuilt, after the furor of the citizens above-noticed had subsided, is uncertain. The comedy of *Woman is a Weathercock*, printed 1612, was acted " diuers times priuately at the White-Friers, by the Children of the Reuels*. Upon July the 13th, 1613, a licence was granted to erect a new play-house. It may therefore be concluded, that if this Theatre was pulled down in 1580, it did not remain long in ruins; and that it could not be from decay that it wanted rebuilding within so short a period, allowing, as the fact might be, that the structure was entirely of timber, but rather from inconvenience of size, to meet the increase of population. However, the new licence was not acted upon until the building of the Salisbury-court Theatre in 1629.

SALISBURY-COURT THEATRE—*Private House, Dorset Court.*—This Theatre was built in 1629. It was usually called a private house; but the meaning of that distinction has not hitherto been explained. The term might be applied to those houses only that were roofed completely over, and which, by discontinuing the inconvenience of an open pit, or yard, served to render the audience more select and respectable. The Blackfriars and the Cockpit in Drury-lane, were also called private-houses; and we are told, the three were all " built almost exactly alike, for form and bigness," had " the pits enclosed for the gentry, and acted by candle-light.†"

The prologue to Marmyon's *Holland's Leagver*, which the title describes " an excellent Comedy, as it hath bin lately and often acted with great applause, by the high and mighty Prince Charles his Seruants, at the Private House, in Salisbury Court," [London,] 1632, [small 4to,] is too incidental to the history of this edifice to be omitted; and, by the commencement of the lines, it appears that the house was first opened by some unsuccessful candidates.

> " Gentle spectators, that with graceful eye
> Come to behold the Muses' colonie,

---

* For an account of the City Prentices attempting to perform here, *The Hog hath lost his Pearl* in 1612-13, see *Reliquiæ Woottonianiæ*, ed. 1685, p. 402.

† Wright's *Historia Histrionica.*

New planted in this soyle ; *forsooke of late*
By the inhabitants, since made fortunate
By more propitious starres ; though on each hand,
To over-top us, two great lawrels stand ;
The one, when she shall please to spread her traine,
The vastness of the GLOBE cannot containe ;
Th' other so high the PHŒNIX does aspire
To build in, and takes new life from the fire
Bright Poesie creates ; yet we partake
The influence they boast of, which does make
Our bayes to flourish, and the leaves to spring,
That on our branches now new poets sing ;
And when with joy hee shall see this resort,
Phœbus shall not disdaine to stile 't his court."

During the memorable period of the Commonwealth, when a multitude of heads, more remembered by brimshades without, than by any proof of sanity within, were ready to combine for the destruction of theatres *en masse,* this house shared the general fate, and remained closed until the Restoration. In June 1660, it was opened hy a newly-gathered company, under the management of the veteran William Beeston ; and in the month of November following, was taken possession of by D'Avenant, whose company probably played there alternately with the Cockpit, until the removal in 1662 to the new Theatre in Portugal-row. The Rump, a comedy, by John Tatham, has in the title of 1660, " acted many times with great applause, at the Private House in Dorset-court ;" and the same play is supposed to have been performed there in 1669.

DORSET-GARDENS THEATRE.—*Duke of York's, or Duke's Theatre, Dorset Gardens—Duke's Theatre, Salisbury Court—Queen's Theatre, Dorset Gardens.*—The house in Portugal-row proving too small, has been considered the reason that Sir William Davenant projected the building a more convenient one in Dorset Gardens, which he was enabled to do, the patent of January 1662-3 granting power to build in " the cities of London and

Westminster, or the suburbs thereof." The design is attributed to Sir Christopher Wren, whose attention might have been directed by Davenant, in his lifetime, to the giving effect to the new scenery ; and therefore this elegant structure was as richly adorned without as within *. The front had a Southern aspect, with a portico, and two smaller arches for the convenience of carriages. The building and scenery cost L.5000. Though this Theatre was probably erected upon nearly the same spot where dramatic exhibitions† had, with only occasional intermissions, existed for near a century, the project was not carried into effect without considerable opposition from the citizens. The voluminous Baxter records this circumstance : " A new playhouse (he says) being built in Salisbury Court, Fleet Street, called the Duke of York's, the Lord Mayor (as it is said) desired of the King that it might not be, the youth of the city being already so corrupted by sensual pleasures ;

* Dryden put in the mouth of the women-actors, in their prologue, when they acted at Lincoln's Inn Fields, to remark,

" The gaudy house with scenes will serve for cits."

Among other fanciful ornaments, there were busts of our principal dramatic writers, which time or the gods, and perhaps both, mutilated. Durfey, in *Collin's Walk through London,* 1690, has given Canto IV. in describing a visit to this play-house, when they performed Ben Jonson's Bartholomew Fair. He says, Collin

" —— saw each box with beauty crown'd,
And pictures deck the structure round ;
Ben, Shakspear, and the learned rout,
With noses some, and some without."

Dryden, whose epigrammatic points in his prologues and epilogues, produced for the other house, were not infrequently to ridicule their rivals, wittily alludes to this exhibition of the Poets in the following couplet of an Epilogue, spoken on opening the new house in Drury-lane, 1674 :—

" Though in their house the poets' heads appear,
We hope we may presume their wits are here."

† That the Salisbury Court Theatre was also called the Dorset Court Theatre, is already shown ; and undoubtedly all three were known as the Whitefriars Theatre. Mr. Malone considers the matter uncertain.

but he obtained not his end.*" It was opened by Davenant's widow, aided by Betterton, at the head of the Duke of York's Company, on the 9th November, 1674, with Dryden's Comedy of " Sir Martin Marall," which was repeated to a full audience for three days, " notwithstanding it had been acted thirty days before in Lincoln's Inn Fields, and above four times at Court†." The novel introduction of Operas‡ and Farces||, and the revival of such stock-pieces as admitted a display of scenery and splendid dresses, proved sufficient to attract a long succession of crowded houses§. Here, in

* *Reliquiæ Baxterianæ*, 1696, Part III.

† Downes's *Roscius Anglicanus*, ed. 1789, p. 41.

‡ As the Empress of Morocco, Psyche, Circe, and Dryden's alteration of the Tempest. In the last the famous comedian Joe Haynes made his appearance as a dancer ; and having learnt in France, " the author of the Tempest (as the biographer of Haynes declares) was obliged to him for the dances which were approved of by the spectators." Thomas's *Life of Haynes*, 1701.

|| I conjecture it was about this period that the actors began to annex a farce occasionally to a short play. When Otway prepared his tragedy of *Titus and Berenice*, with a prologue, for this stage, he added the farce of the *Cheats of Scapin*, and after it an epilogue. Several other farces appear to have been acted here.

§ The following lines, descriptive of the performance, are from Durfey's Poem, already noticed : —

> " Upon the bank of Thame and Isis,
> That feeds the wen of city vices,
> By bearing wealth upon their shoulders,
> To fools, phanaticks, and free-holders ;
> A lofty pile there stands whose use is,
> To nourish and regale the Muses ;
> Not with coarse fare of greasy bits,
> But with rare treats of costly wits ;
> Jelly of tropes and rich potages
> Of rants and high poetick rages ;
> Brisk metaphors they also choose,
> And simile to make raggous,
> Garnisht with leaves of antique books,
> And all the poets are their cooks,

1682, the Embassadour from the Emperour of Morocco was entertained with Psyche, " a play of extraordinary splendour ;" and on other evenings saw Macbeth and the Tempest, and was extremely pleased*. However, the renewal of the embellishments and dresses, although the house was " more frequented than the King's†," proved a pageant too costly in continuance for the actors to derive a competent emolument ; and which circumstance finally led to a junction of the company with their long-continued rivals at Drury-lane. This scheme was formed under an Agreement, dated October the 14th, 1681, between Dr. Davenant, Betterton, and Smith, of the one part ; and Charles Hart, and Edward Kynaston, of the other part: whereby, in consideration of certain pensions, Hart and Kynaston agreed within a month to make over " all the right, title, and claim, which they or either of them had to any Plays, Books, Cloaths, and Scenes in the King's Play-house‡." They also promised to " promote, with all their power and interest, an agree-

> Here empress Tragedy still treads,
> And the grand dance in buskins leads ;
> And farce in vizard mask is seen,
> In mimick garb like Harlequin,
> Deck'd with a nosegay of fresh buds,
> Of prologues, songs, and interludes.
> Here each man's genius is a mirrour,
> Where he may see and fly from error,
> Where every vice uncover'd is,
> And every fop may see his phiz."

---

* A singular occurrence is mentioned in a newspaper as having taken place the 27th April, 1682, when " Mr. Ch[arles] D[eering], son to Sir Edw. D. and Mr. V[aughan] quarrelled in the Duke's play-house, and presently mounted the stage and fought, and Mr. D. was very dangerously wounded, and Mr. V. secured, lest it should prove mortal." *Janeway's Impartial Protestant Mercury*, May 2.—Langbaine relates his beholding a more sanguinary tragedy in 1674, in the pit of this house, " in the death of Mr. Scroop, who received his death's wound from Sir Thomas Armstrong." See *An Account of the Dramatick Poets*, p. 460.

† Langbaine, p. 178.   ‡ Curll's Hist. of the Stage, p. 10.

ment between both play-houses;" and which took effect about July 1682*. On August 10th of that year, they performed the tragedy of Romulus and Hirsilia, or the Sabine War†, with an Epilogue by Mrs. Behn, and spoken by Lady Slingsby‡, which reflecting upon the Duke of Monmouth, the Lord Chamberlain is said to have ordered both ladies into custody, to answer the affront‖.

From the time the companies joined, the performances were continued at both houses alternately; and did not prevent the producing several new pieces at Dorset Garden.

Elkanah Settle, whose versatile genius supplied either opera, city pageant, or Bartholomew-fair droll, was probably the first dramatic writer that sought to extend and support his popularity through the aid of a newspaper; and certainly the following paragraph, from the Post-Boy, is one of the earliest, if not the first, dramatic puffs which appeared through the medium of such a circulation! it was inserted a few days before the performance of *The World in the Moon*. "Great preparations are making for a new OPERA, in the play-house in *Dorset Garden*, of which there is great expectation, the scenes being several new sets, and of a moddel different from

---

* Early in August, the Duchess of York visited the Duke's Theatre, " that and the King's House having joined interests," to see " Virtue Betrayed, or Anna Bullen, a deep tragedy of the beheading the said Lady by King Henry the Eighth." *London Mercury*, Aug. 8, 1682.

† There was advertised to " be published on Monday next, the last new play, called Romulus," &c. in Brooks's *Impartial Mercury* of Friday, Nov. 17, 1682. The incident above-noticed probably occasioned a delay in the printing.

‡ Her " name occurs as Lady Slingsby in the *Dramatis Personæ* of Dryden and Lee's plays, between the years 1681 and 1689. In 1680 she appears as Mrs. Mary Lee. Her name was originally Aldridge. Who her husband was is not known." *Lysons's Environs*, vol. III. p. 367.—It is probable her husband was a Justice of Peace, acting in the County of Middlesex, as I believe the name occurs repeatedly about that time in the parish accounts of St. Clement's Danes.

‖ Curtis's Protestant Mercury, Aug. 16, 1682.

all that have been used in any theatre whatever, being twice as high as any of their former scenes ; and the whole decorations of the stage not only infinitely beyond all the Operas ever yet performed in *England*, but also by the acknowledgment of several gentlemen that have travell'd abroad, much exceeding all that has been seen on any of the Foreign stages*." However, notwithstanding the attraction of a new Opera, with the novelty of enlarged scenery, and the auxiliary aid just noticed, this piece proved little more than a requiem to the theatrical performances at this house, which appear to have finally terminated with the season of 1696-7†.

In the following year a penny lottery was drawn here, as is shown by a tract, intituled " The Wheel of Fortune, or Nothing for a Penny ; being remarks on the drawing of the Penny Lottery at the Theatre-Royal, in Dorset Gardens," 1698, 4to. Afterwards there was a short exhibition of prize-fighters ; and the building was totally deserted in 1703.‡

---

* The Post Boy, June 12-15,1697. On the 24th was advertised that " to-morrow will be published the new opera called The World in the Moon." And upon Thursday, July 1st, appeared the following paragraph ; " The new Opera will be acted this day for the benefit of the undertaker." Upon the same day the publisher advertised ; " The New Opera, called the World in the Moon, is acting with great applause. It is licensed by the Lord Chamberlain's Secretary, and the Master of the Revels ; and may be had with all the songs, at A. Roper's, at the Blackboy in Fleet-Street, price 1s." The second edition, by E. S. was announced March 17th 1697-8.

† In that plot-creating age, a rumour was raised against the players, as we are told in the Protestant Mercury of Sept. 23, 1696, that " yesterday morning the play-house in Salisbury-court was beset by musqueteers, and searched by messengers ;" but the report was afterwards declared to be erroneous.

‡ " By this time (says my author) we were come to our propos'd landing-place, where a stately edifice (the front supported by lofty columns) presented to our view. I enquired of my friend, what magnanimous Don *Cressus* resided in that noble and delightful mansion? Who told me, nobody as he knew on, except rats and mice ; and perhaps an old superannuated *Jack pudding*, to look after it, and to take care that no decay'd lover of the Drama should get in, and steal away the *poets pictures*, and sell em to some Upholsterers, for *Roman Emperours* I suppose ; there being little else to lose except scenes, machines, or some such jim-cracks. For this, says he, is one of the theaters, but wholly abandon'd by the players ; and 'tis thought

This playhouse is generally described as " the Duke's Theatre, Dorset Gardens ;" the checks had a double D, one being reversed with the letter Y central, surmounted by a ducal coronet, obverse " Vpper Gallerie, 1671." The second title above-cited is used in the Agreement to promote the union of the two companies; and the actors were distinguished as "their Royal Highnesses' Servants" contra " their Majesties' servants," who acted at Drury-lane. In February, 1684–5, upon the accession to the throne of the Duke of York, this house was immediately distinguished as " the Queen's Theatre." In compliment to the patroness, new checks were cast, preserving the date according to the old stile. On one side, in bass-relief, is the head of Maria d'Este with " Qveen's Theatre," obverse, " forthe Pit 1684," and are of yellow metal. Similar ones " for the First Gallerie, 1684," and " Vpper Gallerie, 1684," The name was not afterwards altered. The frontispiece to Elkanah Settle's *Empress of Morocco* is a front view of this Theatre, having, when perfect, some Latin lines beneath.* There is also a bird's-eye view, taken in the same direction, in Walker's plan of London, published by Overton, as " the old play-house."

VERE STREET THEATRE.—A large portion of Vere-street, Clare-market, and the adjoining neighbourhood, was built on land called St. Clement's fields ; and one of the earliest erections was a bowling alley and tennis court, situate in Bear-yard ; a name which is still continued, and leaves no

---

will in a little time be pull'd down, if it is not bought by some of the dissenting brethren, and converted into a more pious use, that might in part atone for the sundry transgressions occasioned by that levity which the stage of late have been so greatly subject to." *The London Spy*, by Edw. Ward, 1703, p. 148.

* There are also scene prints, which show the internal magnificence of the house. Previous to that publication, the principal dramatic pieces that had any embellishment were Jack Jugler, Somebody and Nobody, The Valiant Welchman, The Roaring Girl, and Jack Drum's Entertainment, each having an incidental woodcut.—The views of Dorset Gardens Theatre, both external and internal, have been copied for the *Londina Illustrata*, but are inadvertently supposed to represent a different building.

doubt the premises were occasionally used for the once popular diversion of bear-baiting. The tennis-court communicated with Vere-street by a passage, according to repute, near where the Bull's-head is now situate, and where Charles Gibbons, Esq. (as he is styled in the parish books) the proprietor, then resided. In 1660 there was erected on the site of the tennis-court, a small Theatre, being the first built after the Restoration; and on Thursday, November 8th, in that year, it was opened with the play of Henry the IVth, by the Company from the Red Bull under the direction of Thomas Killigrew.

One event has given some importance to this Theatre, in the history of the drama. Mr. Malone, with a discrimination not easy to be controverted, supposes that here, on Saturday, Dec. 6, 1660, upon the performance of Othello, the first time that season, " it is probable an Actress first appeared on the English Stage."* Though the prologue and epilogue spoken on the occasion are in print,† yet the name of this heroine is not preserved.

At this house, Killigrew's Company continued during the seasons of 1661, 1662, and part of 1663; and within that period obtained the title of " The Kinge and Queen's Company of Players." In the latter year, they removed to the new-built Theatre in Drury-lane; and it does not appear that this house was again used for dramatic representations. Davenant, who shortly

---

* Masques and Pastorals were frequently represented at Court by the Queen of Charles I. and her Ladies. Prynne, when defending himself against the Prelates' tyranny, states that her Majesty acted a part in a pastoral at Somerset-house about six weeks after the publishing the *Histrio-Mastix,* when the Archbishop of Canterbury and the Prelates produced the book upon the following morning to the King; and having shewn that the table of reference called " women actors notorious whores," they declared that he had purposely written the book " against the Queene and her pastorall." And in a marginal note Prynne relates the following anecdote: " Mr. H. I. that first presented and shewed the booke to the King, was a few moneths after committed prisoner to the Tower, for begetting one of the actors of this pastorall with child soone after it was acted, and making a reall commentary on M. Prynne's misapplyed text, both the actresse and he for this cause becomming M. Prynne's fellow prisoners in the Tower." See *A New Discovery of the Prelates' Tyranny,* &c. 1641, 4to.

† Reed's Shakspeare, vol. III. p. 135.

afterwards produced his *Play-house to lett,* alludes to it by making a Musician say,

" —————————— Rest you merry ;
There is another play house to let in *Vere Street."*

Probably it remained unoccupied until Mr. Ogilby, the author of " Itinerarium Angliæ, or Book of Roads," adopted it, as standing in a popular neighbourhood,* for the temporary purpose of drawing a Lottery of Books, which took place in 1668 ;† and it was then, to distinguish it from the two neighbouring edifices in Little Lincoln's-inn-fields, and Drury-lane, called the " Old Theatre." By another transition we find the volatile players suc-

---

* In addition to the houses inhabited by the Nobility, &c. in Drury-lane and neighbourhood, the " New Market," now called " Clare-Market," had been recently established.

† As the Lotteries were connected with the Theatres and Literature in more than one instance, it may not be out of place to give here a brief notice of their progress. They were instituted by patent soon after the Restoration, for the purpose of creating a fund for the suffering Loyalists, and books were often the species of property held out as a lure for the adventurer. Among these Blome's Recreations, and Gwillim's Heraldry, first edition, may be mentioned. In the Gazette of May 18, 1668, is the following advertisement : " Mr. Ogilby's Lottery of Books opens on Monday the 25th instant, at the Old Theatre, between Lincoln's-inn fields and Vere-street ; where all persons concerned may repair on Monday, May 18, and see the Volumes, and put in their money." On May 25th is announced. " Mr. Ogilby's Lottery of Books (adventures comming in so fast that they cannot in so short time be methodically registered) opens not till Tuesday the 2d of June : then not failing to draw ; at the Old Theatre between Lincoln's-inn field and Vere-street."—The letters patent were from time to time renewed, and by those dated June 19, and Dec. 17, 1674, there was granted for thirteen years to come, " all Lotteries whatsoever, invented or to be invented, to several truly loyal and indigent officers in consideration of their many faithful services and sufferings, with prohibition to all others to use or set up the said Lotteries," unless deputations were obtained from those officers. Gazette, Oct. 11, 1675. Of all the schemes the most popular one was that drawn at the Dorset-garden Theatre, with the capital prize of a thousand pound for a penny. The drawing began Oct. 19, 1698 ; and in the *Protestant Mercury* of the following day " its fairness (was said) to give universal content to all that were concerned." In the next paper is found an inconsistent and frivolous story as to the possessor of the prize : " Some time since a

ceeded by the austere puritans.   In 1675 the parish rates paid by the widow
Gibbons (whose husband had been dead several years) are entered for " the
Tennis Court;" which might be an error of the Collector, who could not
but remember " such things were," as in the following year it is fitly described as " The Meeting-house."   The same title is used in 1682, when, in
consequence of an order in Council for the suppressing conventicles, several
attempts were made by the constables to take into custody the preachers who
held forth at the " old play-house in Vere-street."

The building must have been very substantial, as, reputedly, it was the
same as that destroyed by fire in 1809.*

THE ROSE.—This Theatre stood on the Bank-side, Southwark.   It was
built before 1590, and was favourably supported by the public, being succes-
sively occupied, from 1591 to 1601, by the respective companies of the Lord

---

boy near Branford going to school one morning, met an old woman, who asked his charity ;
the boy replied, he had nothing to give her but a piece of bread and butter, which she accepted.
Some time after, she met the boy again, and told him she had good luck after his bread and
butter, and therefore would give him a penny, which, after some years keeping, would produce
many pounds : he accordingly kept it a great while ; and at last, with some friend's advice,
put into it the Penny Lottery, and we are informed that on Tuesday last the said lot came up
with L.1000 prize."   However absurd this relation appears, it must be recollected those to
whom it was principally addressed, had given proof of having sufficient credulity for such a
tale, in believing that two hundred and forty thousand shares could be disposed of and appropriated to a single number independent of other prizes.   The scheme was afterwards attacked
in a pamphlet already noticed, (p. 96.) which was not sufficient to prevent a further attempt
at a fraud upon the public.   In 1698-9, schemes were started, called " the Lucky Adventure ;
or, Fortunate Chance, being L.2000 for a groat, or L.3000 for a shilling," and Fortunatus, or
another adventure of L.1000 for a penny :" but purchasers were more wary, and the money
returned in both cases.—The patentees also advertised against the " Marble-board, alias the
Woollwich-board lotteries ; the Figure-board, alias the Whimsey-board, and the Wyre-board
lotteries."   This nefarious system was finally closed by Act of Parliament, in the 10th and
11th of William III. c. 17, which declared them unlawful after 29th Dec. 1699.

* For a View of the ruins, see the *Londina Illustrata,* where it is called " the Duke's
Theatre."

Strange, the Earl of Sussex, the Lord Admiral, and the Earl of Pembroke. In 1613 it was entirely forsaken, and only re-opened about seven years afterwards, for a short duration, with an exhibition of Prize-fighters.

THE HOPE.—Also built on the Bank-side, and where the servants of Lady Elizabeth exhibited in 1613. At this Theatre was first produced the " Bartholomew fair" of Ben Jonson, which impresses us with a favourable opinion of the dramatic performances, though a prevailing fashion for ruder exhibitions afterwards served to convert the premises into a Bear-garden ; for which purpose they were in use in 1632.

THE SWAN.—Another of the Bank-side Theatres, where the actors occasionally resorted. It is spoken of as shut in 1613, but afterwards served for exhibitions of Prize-fighting until 1632, when it had fallen into a general decay, as appears by a tract printed in that year, called " *Holland's Leaguer.*" *The Hope* and *the Swan* are described as standing very near *the Globe*, and forming three famous Amphitheatres. That " one (says the writer) was the *Continent of the world*, because half the year a world of beauties and brave spirits resorted unto it ; the other was a building of excellent *Hope*, and though wild beasts and gladiators did most possess it, yet the gallants that came to behold those combats, though they were of a mixed society, yet were many noble worthies amongst them ; the last which stood, being in times past as famous as any of the other, was now fallen to decay, and like a dying *Swan*, hanging down her head, seemed to sing her own dirge."*

Sadler's Musick-house, Islington.—Miles's Musick-house.—Sadler's Wells. —Soon after the Revolution, upon the Drama being emancipated from the rigid shackles of the Puritans, a novel species of amusement first became

---

* A pleasing print of the Swan Theatre, taken from the long view of London called the " Antwerp view," is inserted in the " Londina Illustrata."

general, under the name of Musick-houses*.   Not one of them, and they
were many, particularly in the Suburbs of the Metropolis, appears to have
attained and preserved the celebrity of Sadler's Musick-house, which was a
wooden building, erected on the North side of the New-river-head at Islington some time before 1683.   In that year, the servants of the proprietor,
Sadler, while digging for gravel in his garden, discovered a well of mineral
water, which is stated to have become in such general repute from its medicinal qualities, as to be visited, shortly afterwards, by " five or six hundred
people every morning." That number is mentioned in an account of the discovery of the Well, given in a note below †; but it was probably a time-ser-
ving puff, to invite the real or fanciful valetudinarian, it being then fashion-

* One of the earliest was Coleman's Musick-house near the Lamb's Conduit ; and that was
to be sold or let in March 1681-2.   It was the custom for women of the most abandoned description to frequent the Musick-houses in Rosemary-lane, Stepney, and other places ; which
became the nightly scenes of intoxication, riots, and even murder.   In 1699 the Peace-officers
made repeated searches in Stepney parish, and in one night took into custody " about forty
couple of suspicious persons, who were all committed."—*Protestant Mercury, March* 29, 1699.

† The following Tract has been partially referred to by Sir John Hawkins, Lysons, and
Strutt ; and the extract now given shows the situation of the Spring, which has been imper-
fectly described by those writers :—

" A true and exact Account of Sadler's Well ; or, the new Mineral Waters lately found at
Islington : treating of its nature and virtues.   Together with an enumeration of the
chiefest Diseases which it is good for, and against which it may be used ; and the manner
and order of taking of it.   Published for public good, by T. G. Doctor of Physick.
London, printed for Thomas Malthus, at the Sun in the Poultry, 1684.

" The new Well at Islington (says the writer) is a certain spring in the middle of a garden,
belonging to the Musick-house, built by Mr. —— Sadler, on the North side of the great
Cistern that receives the New River water near Islington ; the water whereof was, before the
Reformation, very much famed for several extraordinary cures performed thereby, and was
thereupon accounted sacred, and called Holy-well.   The Priests belonging to the Priory of
Clarken-well using to attend there, made the people believe, that the virtues of the waters proceeded from the efficacy of their prayers.   But, upon the Reformation, the Well was stopt up,
upon a supposition that the frequenting it was altogether superstitious ; and so, by degrees, it
grew out of remembrance, and was wholly lost until found out, and the fame of it revived again,
by the following accident : Mr. Sadler being made surveyor of the highways, and having good
Gravel in his own Garden, employed two men to dig there ; and when they had dug pretty

able to resort to all such places, either in hope of relief, or for amusement*.

deep, one of them found his pickaxe strike upon something that was very hard ; whereupon he endeavoured to break it, but could not ; whereupon, thinking with himself that it might peradventure be some treasure hid there, he uncovered it very carefully, and found it to be a broad flat stone ; which having loosened and lifted up, he saw it was supported by four oaken posts, and had under it a large Well of stone, arched over, and curiously carved : and having viewed it, he called his fellow-labourer to see it likewise, and asked him whether they should fetch Mr. Sadler and shew it him? Who, having no kindness for Sadler, said No ; he should not know of it, but as they had found it so they would stop it up again, and take no notice of it ; which he that found it consented to at first, but, after a little time, he found himself (whether out of curiosity or some other reason, I shall not determine) strongly inclined to tell Sadler of the Well, which he did one Sabbath-day in the evening. Sadler, upon this, went down to see the Well ; and observing the curiosity of the stone-work that was about it, and fancying within himself that it was a Medicinal water, formerly had in great esteem, but by some accident or other lost, he took some of it in a bottle, and carried it to an eminent Physician, telling him how the Well was found out, and desiring his judgment of the water ; who having tasted and tried it, told him it was very strong of a Mineral taste, and advised him to brew some Beer with it, and carry it to some persons, to whom he would recommend him : which he did accordingly. And some of those who used to have it of him in bottles, found so much good by it, that they desired him to bring it in Roundlets : which was done most part of the last winter, and continued to have so good an effect upon the persons that drank it, that, at the beginning of this summer, Dr. Morton advised several of his patients to drink the water ; which had so good an effect upon them, and operates so near Tunbridge Water, that it has obtained a general approbation, and great numbers of those who used to go thither, drink it. There are few Physicians in London but have advised some or other of their patients to drink it ; by which means it is so frequented, that there are five or six hundred people there constantly every morning."

After describing the effects of the water, the diseases to be relieved, and the manner of taking it, the patients are informed that they may eat caraways, or drink a glass of rhenish, or white wine with it ; and that " it is very convenient for those who smoke tobacco, to take a pipe or two whilst their waters work."

* At the time the discovery was made by Sadler, the Wells at Tunbridge and Epsom had long been places of fashionable resort. The Ebbisham, or Epsom water, was discovered in 1630, or soon after, and supposed to be the first, of its peculiar quality, discovered in England, In the Prologue to " The Empress of Morocco [by Elkanah Settle, 4to,]," 1673, the Poet says :

" All you're now like to have is a dull play,
The Wells have stol'n the vizar masks away :
Now Punk in penitential drink begins,
To purge the surfeit of her London sins."

How long Sadler resided there after the discovery is uncertain.   The building

Both places were also made the subjects of Comedies, and were so numerously frequented, that, in the Gazette of June 19, 1684, it is announced, " that the Post will go every day (to and fro) betwixt London and Tunbridge, and also betwixt London and Epsom, during the season for drinking those waters." We shall notice a few that have flourished within the environs of London.

The *Clerks Well*, which now gives name to the populous neighbourhood and parish of Clerkenwell, is the most antient of those in the vicinity of the Metropolis. It is indebted for its fame to the history of the Drama, as will be noticed hereafter, and not to any medicinal virtues in the Spring.

Hampstead Wells were discovered about 1698, and the water sold for three-pence a flask. There was a concert every Monday at 10 o'clock, and the ticket of admission one shilling, and for dancing in the afternoon sixpence. They flourished several years, and their history, we may expect, will be copiously given in the forthcoming " History of Hampstead," by Mr J. J. Park. [Published, Lond. 1814. roy. 8vo.]

Islington Wells, now called Islington Spa, or New Tunbridge Wells. This place was in repute at the time of Sadler's discovery of the Well in the land adjoining, and which last being long since closed, has led some of our best writers to describe the Islington Spa as that found by Sadler. By a singular advertisement in the Gazette of September 1685, it appears to have been then recently sold : it commences, " Whereas Mr. John Langley of London, Merchant, who bought the Rhinoceros, and Islington Wells, hath been represented by divers of his malitious adversaries to be a person of no estate or reputation, nor able to discharge his debts," &c. At the time Ward wrote his Poem, describing this place, three-pence a piece admission was paid at " a gate, where abundance of rabble peept in at a grate." He afterwards says,

" Lime-trees were plac'd at a regular distance,
And *Scrapers* were giving their woful assistance."

However, Musick was not originally part of the plan, though there was a Coffee-house attached to the premises. This may be gleaned from the advertisements in 1690—1692, only informing the publick, " That the Well near Islington, called New Tunbridge," would open " for drinking the Medicinal Waters, where the poor may have the same, gratis, bringing a Certificate under the hand of any known Physician or Apothecary." In 1700, there was " Musick for dancing all day long every Monday and Thursday during the summer season. No mask to be admitted :" and, in 1733, it was visited by the late Princess Amelia for the purpose of drinking the waters. It also furnished a Tale to a Dramatic trifle by the late George Colman, called " The Spleen, or Islington Spa," acted at Drury-lane in 1776 ; and in the following year, the proprietor, Mr. Holland, declared in an advertisement, the number of Patients daily receiving benefit, " scarcely to be credited." It was then let on lease ; and upon the failure of

in 1699 was called Miles's Musick-house, though the water was advertised
Holland, an unexpired term of thirteen years was sold by Mr. Skinner in September 1778.
The new Proprietors gave notice in the following month, that the Gardens were open every
Morning for drinking the Waters, and in the Afternoon for Tea. " The subscription for the
Season one guinea; non-subscribers drinking the Waters 6*d.* each morning." These regulations continued to the final close of the Gardens. A few years since, an attempt was made to
establish a Minor Vauxhall; and during one of the late Seasons of Lent, there was an Orrery
exhibited, with Evening Lectures. The Coffee-house has been lately pulled down, and a row
of houses built upon part of the Gardens, but the Well continues open for the benefit of the
publick. There is a pleasing view of this place engraved by G. Bickham, jun. in a folio
Volume of Songs, published about 1737, and shows the Company waiting round the quadrangle
of the Balustrades enclosing the Well, to be served; others walking in the Gardens, which
were irregularly planted with trees; and in the perspective appears the House and Coffee-room.
The View forms a Head-piece to the following Song, taken from " The Humours of New
Tunbridge Wells," a Lyric Poem, written by Mr. Lockman in 1733. See Gent. Mag. vol·
IV. p. 99 and 111.

The Charms of Dishabille, or new Tunbridge Wells at Islington.

" Whence comes it that the shining Great,
To titles born and awful state,
        Thus condescend, thus check their will,
And send away to Tunbridge Wells,
To mix with vulgar Beaux and Belles?
Ye sages, your famed glasses raise,
Survey this meteor's dazzling blaze,
        And say, portends it good, or ill?

Soon as Aurora gilds the skies
With brighter charms the Ladies rise,
        To dart from beams that save or kill,
No homage at the toilett paid,
(Their lovely features unsurvey'd)
Sweet Negligence her influence lends,
And all the artless graces blends,
        That form the tempting Dishabille.

Behold the walks, a chequer'd shade,
In the gay pride of green array'd;

O

How bright the Sun! the Air how still !
In wild confusion there we view,
Red ribbons groop'd with aprons blew,
Scrapes, curtzies, nods, winks, smiles, and frowns ;
Lords, milkmaids, dutchesses, and clowns,
          In their all-various Dishabille.

Thus in the famous Age of Gold,
(Not quite romantick tho' so old)
          Mankind were merely Jack and Gill :
On flow'ry banks by murmuring streams,
They tatl'd, walk'd, had pleasing dreams ;
But dress'd, indeed, like aukward folks,
Not steeple-hats, surtouts, short cloaks,
          Fig-leaves the only Dishabille."

Richmond Wells.   First discovered about 1680 ; and in the Post Boy of July 11, 1696, was announced, " At Richmond New Wells, a Consort of Musick both vocal and instrumental, will be performed on Monday next, at Noon, the 13th instant, by principal hands, and the best voices, composed new for the day, by Mr. Frank ; the Songs will be printed and sold there." This was probably, the first public opening of the Wells ; and " a great concourse of persons of quality" being there, " it was desired the rate at coming in should be doubled, viz. to make it 6*d.* each." Such was the tenor of the advertisement in the following week ; and the two following confirm the patronage and celebrity of this place. " At the desire of several persons of quality, Mr. Abell will sing on Monday, the 11th of this instant August, at 5 of the clock precisely, in the great room at the Wells at Richmond, it being the last time of his singing this season, and will perform in English, Latin, Italian, Spanish, and French, accompanied with instrumental musick, by the best masters ; and after that, will sing alone to the Harpsichord.   The usual dancing will begin at eight of the clock, price five shilling each ticket.   Note, That the tyde of flood begins at one of the clock in the afternoon, and flows till five, and ebbs till twelve, for the conveniency of returning.   Tickets will be had at the Wells, and no where else."—*Postman, August* 9, 1701. " At Richmond Wells, on Thursday next, being the 12th instant, at the request of several persons of quality, will be a great Consort of Musick ; Mr. Elford and Mr. Weldon will perform several new songs, all composed on purpose for this entertainment, by the said Mr. Weldon.   Some of the songs to be accompanied with a flute, by Mr. Peasible ; and a new symphony for a flute and a violin, by him and the famous Signor Gasparini, who will perform several Italian Sonatas, accompanied by Mr. De Par, and other great symphonies, by the best masters ; beginning exactly at 5, and to end at 7, because of the dancing after.

5s. a ticket, to be had at White's Chocolate-house and Garroway's Coffee-house. This Consort to be performed but once, the Queen going to the Bath. Tide serves at 7 o'clock in the morning, and light nights."—*Postman, Aug.* 10, 1703. This place was in considerable repute for near half a century, rapidly declining after 1750.

Lambeth Wells consisted of two Wells, distinguished as the *nearer* and *farther* Well. They were open before 1697. On the 5th of May, in that year, was first performed a Concert in imitation of the regular one, then newly established, in York Buildings, and by the following Advertisement was continued weekly: " In the great Room at Lambeth Wells (every Wednesday for the ensuing Season) will be performed a Concert of vocal and instrumental Musick, consisting of about thirty instruments and voices, after the method of the Musick-meeting in York Buildings, the price only excepted, each person being to pay for coming in but one shilling; to begin at half an hour after two, and no person to be admitted after three." The hour was soon afterwards altered to six, and no person to be admitted in a Mask. In 1700, the price of admission was reduced to three-pence a-piece, as *formerly:* the water was then sold at a penny a quart, and the poor had it gratis. About 1740, the Wells became neglected, and the Musick-room a nuisance, which thereupon passed to the possession of the Methodists.

Streatham Wells. Well known as early as 1660. There was a Concert upon Monday and Thursday in every week during the Summer of 1701; but it was never a place of distinguished resort except to drink the water.

Acton Wells are mentioned under the date of 1612: and were in considerable repute about the middle of last century. Assemblies were held there during the Season; and in 1775, the proprietor, Mr. Gardner, acknowledged, in the papers of the day, the patronage giving by the subscribers to the public breakfasts.

Bagnigge Wells. Upon the Eastern banks of a very narrow stream, or brook, now little better than a ditch, though heretofore called *The River Bagnigg*, was an antient building, as appears by the following inscription: " S. T. This is Bagnigge-house neare the Pinder a Wakefeilde, 1680." This House was the country residence of Nell Gwynn, one of the favourites of King Charles the IInd; and here is an effigy of that Lady in carved work, with fruits of all sorts about her, gilt, and in good preservation. It was a Chimney-piece, and supposed to allude to her origin of selling fruit at the play-houses. About 1760, upon the discovery of two Mineral Springs, the House and Gardens were opened for public reception, and, probably from the above meretricious connection, called " The Royal Bagnigge Wells." The waters were drank at three-pence each person, or delivered at the pump-room at eight-pence a gallon. As a place of public resort upon a Sunday, the Gardens are well known; and for the amusement of the visitors during the week, there is an excellent Organ in the long room. A curious Mezzotinto print of Bagnigge Wells was published by J. R. Smith in 1772.—Since this article was put to press, the whole of the Furniture, &c. was sold by auction by order of the Assignees of Mr. Salter (the tenant) a Bankrupt. The fixture and fittings-up are described as comprizing " the erections of a temple, a grotto, alcoves, arbours, boxes, green-house, paling-fences, large lead figures, pumps, cisterns, sinks, pipes, (and also) counters, beer-machine, stoves, coppers, partitions, garden lights, shrubs, 200 drinking tables, 350 forms, 400 dozen bottled ale," &c. The sale took place the 16th, 17th, and 18th of December.

Pancras Wells. From a South prospect of this place, engraved by Toms, there appears to have been a public room sixty feet long and eighteen feet high, two pump-houses, and the house of entertainment, 135 feet long, besides gardens, &c. The Wells were numerously attended when in fashion ; and the water had not only the recommendation of being very grateful to the taste, but might be taken in any season.

Kilburn Wells. At the time of publishing the " Outlines of the Natural History of Great Britain and Ireland, by John Berkenhout, M. D. 1772," these Wells had not attracted the notice of any writer upon the Mineral waters ; although, in the following year they appear to have " been in the utmost perfection, the gardens enlarged, and greatly improved, the great room being particularly adapted to the use and amusement of the politest companies, fit either for musick, dancing, or entertainment."—*Advertisement, July* 1773.

St. George's Spa, or Dog and Duck. The Spring was discovered about 1750—60, and, as a public Tea-garden, was within a few years past, a favourite resort for the vilest dregs of society, until properly suppressed by the Magistrates. The site forms part of the ground taken by the Governors for the New Bethlem Hospital.

In addition to the above places where amusement and fashion attached a local celebrity to the different Wells, there may be added the names of several Chalybeate and other Springs, which, although totally depending on their Medicinal virtues, have obtained considerable repute, and are also situate in the vicinity of London. As *Sydenham, Dulwich, or Lewisham Wells,* discovered about the year 1640 ; *Barnet Wells,* known about the middle of the 17th century, and repaired within a few years past ; *Northall Wells,* certainly known before 1690 ; *Woodford Wells,* no longer in estimation ; *Shadwell Spa,* strongly recommended by a pamphlet in 1749 ; *St. Chad's Well, near Battle Bridge,* which still retains its admirers ; lastly, in the same neighbourhood, may be mentioned the spring or conduit on the Eastern side of the road leading from Clerkenwell by Bagnigge Wells, and which has given name to a very few small houses as *Black Mary's Hole.* The land here was formerly called Bagnigg Marsh, from the river Bagnigg which passes through it. But in after-time the citizens resorting to drink the waters of the conduit, which was then leased to one Mary, who kept a black cow, whose milk the gentlemen and ladies drank with the waters of the conduit, from whence, the wits of that age used to say : " Come let us go to Mary's black hole." However, Mary dying, and the place degenerating into licentiousness, about 1687, Walter Baynes, Esq. of the Inner Temple, enclosed the Conduit in the manner it now is, which looks like a great oven. He is supposed to have left a Fund for keeping same in perpetual repair. The stone, with the inscription, was carried away during the night, about ten years ago. The from 1697 unto 1700, and later, in the name of Sadler*. A description of the company frequenting this place, not much to its advantage in the colouring, at the same time with a delineation too minute to doubt the faithfulness of the outline, is given in the dramatic piece intituled " The Weekly Comedy,

water (which formerly fed two ponds on the other side the road) falls into the old Bagnigge river.

The River of Wells. In Pancras parish, at the foot of Hampstead Hill, is the rise, spring, or head of the antient river of Wells, which has its influx into the Thames. After its passage through the fields between Pond-street and Kentish-town, washing the West of that village, it passes to Pancras, and from thence by several meanders through Battle-bridge, Black Mary's-hole, Hockley-in-the-hole, Turnmill-street, Field-lane, Holborn-bridge to Fleet-ditch. Of this River, tradition saith, that it was once navigable, and that lighters and barges used to go up as far as Pancras Church ; and that in digging, anchors have been found within these two hundred years : hence by the choaking up of the river, it is easy to account for the decay of the town of Pancras. In the Speculum Britanniæ, Norden mentions, there were, formerly, many buildings about Pancras Church then decayed, and from the great valley, observable from Holborn-bridge to Pancras : it is probable it was once flooded.—In the neighbourhood of Clerkenwell, there were several others, as Skinner's Well, Fag's Well, Tode Well, Loder's Well, and Radwell : and the overflowing of all these, according to Stow, once fell into that river ; and hence it was called the River of Wells.

* The following Advertisement appeared in the Post-boy, and also the Flying Post, June 1697 :—" Sadler's excellent Steel Waters at Islington, having been obstructed for some years past, are now opened and currant again, and the waters are found to be in their full vigour, strength, and vertue, as ever they were, as is attested and assured by the Physicians, who have since fully tried them. They have been for several years known and experimented to be very effectual for the cure of all hectick and hypocondriacal heat, for beginning consumptions, for melancholy distempers, the scurvy, diabetes, for bringing away gravel, stones in the kidnies and bladder, and several other diseases. The Well will be opened on Monday next, being the 21st instant."

In the Postman of April 27, 1700 :—" These are to give notice, that Sadler's last found Wells at Islington (highly approved of and recommended by Dr. Lower and other eminent Physicians, as the great quantity of Crocus Martis in them, shew they exceed most Chalybeat springs) are now fixing, and recommended to the tryal of other ingenious persons for the good of the publick." Again, on October 9th, it commences, " The proprietors of Sadler's last found Mineral Wells at Islington," &c.

as it is daily acted at most Coffeehouses in London*," with a truly disgusting relation of a fellow eating a live cock at this place ; which had occasioned " abundance of Inns of Court Beaus, and Lady Bumsitters, mingled with
an innumerable swarm of the blew-frock order, to flock into Mile's Musick-
house."

Whatever celebrity the spring obtained on its first discovery, it appears
within a short period to have fallen into disuse, as Ward, in a narrative
poem called " A Walk to Islington, with a description of New Tunbridge
Wells and Sadler's Musick-house†," gives the fame of the Wells to its Medicinal water, and of the Musick-house to such good cheer as cheese-cakes,
custards, bottled ale and cider, and the diversions of singing and dancing.
From this writer may be gleaned some account of the performers and amusements, which are described in his customary strain of low sarcastic humour.
Upon entering, he ascends to the gallery adjoining the organ-loft, the front
of which was painted with the stories of Apollo and Daphne, Jupiter and
Europa, &c. and which seems to have been appropriated to the genteel part
of the company, as, on looking over to " examine the pit," he notices as present, " butchers, bailiffs, prize-fighters, deer-stealers, buttocks and files," and

---

* The Weekly Comedy was published periodically, in half sheets, folio, and the first Number appeared about May 3, 1699. It is by Edward Ward ; and the same piece as was afterwards inserted in his Miscellaneous Works, as *the Humours of a Coffee-house.* The story
was related in the 3d Number of the play which was published Wednesday, May the
24th ; and in *Dawks's Protestant Mercury* of same date is the following paragraph : " London,
May 24. On Wednesday last a fellow at Sadler's Wells, near Islington, after he had dined
heartily on a buttock of beef, for the lucre of five guineas, eat a live cock, feathers, guts and
all, with only a plate of oil and vinegar for sawce, and half a pint of brandy to wash it down :
and afterwards proffered to lay a wager of five guineas more, that he could do the same again
in two hours time. This is attested by many credible people, who were eye-witnesses of the
same : which makes me think of the by-word, *That cook ruffian scalded the Devil in his
feathers,* and I think that food fittest for such a guest." In the same Paper, of January 24,
following, this monster is stated to have eat a live cat at Musick-house in St. Katherine's.

† Probably printed as early as the Weekly Comedy, and afterwards inserted in Ward's
Miscellaneous Works 1703 ; again, 1717, 8vo.

" vermin trained up to the gallows." However, to this rude assemblage, musick had charms ; for the appearance of " Lady Squab," in her old place by the organ, soon obtained silence, and

> " If the ravishing song which she sang you wou'd know,
> It was *Rub, rub, rub, rub, rub, rub, in and out ho.*"

The next in succession was a fiddler, dressed in scarlet ; but, our humorist declares, unlike an Orpheus, and fierce as Mars ; adding,

> " He runs up in *alt,* with Hey diddle diddle,
> To shew what a fool he could make of a fiddle."

There next came a damsel, of the age of eleven, who performed a sword-dance :

> " Arm'd Amazon like, with abundance of rapiers,
> Which she puts to her throat, as she dances and capers ;
> And further the Mob's admiration to kindle,
> She turns on her heel like a wheel on a spindle ;
> And under her petticoats gathers such wind,
> That fans her and cools her before and behind."

The performance was continued by a " young babe of grace," who danced a jig, and diverted the audience with " making strange musick-house monkey-like faces." The conclusion was a dance by " honest friend Thomas," who supported the two-fold character of clown and waiter, and is treated with lenity by the poet, because he filled " good Nantz."

The same description of low, disorderly characters, continued to make this a place of rendezvous for several years. There is a rare tract called " God's Judgment against Murderers ; or, an account of a cruel and barbarous Murther, committed on Thursday night the 14th of August, at Sadler's Musick-house, near Islington, on the body of Mr. Waite, a Lieutenant of a Man of War, by one Mr. French, a Lawyer of the Temple, shewing how they quarrelled about women," &c. 1712. One passage is too incidental for omission :

" This famous place (says the writer) called Sadler's Wells, otherwise Miles's Musick-house, is so well known to most people in Town, that I need not describe it. It is a daily meeting or rendezvous of people who go thither to divert themselves ; and though 'tis in many very innocent, and in the people of the house, only getting an honest livelihood ; yet the method of so doing is apt to draw many unaccountable and disorderly persons to frequent it, under the colour of diverting themselves."

Miles, who, by improving and beautifying, added to the popularity of the Musick-house, was succeeded by Frances Forcer, the son of the musician, who is supposed to have occupied the premises after Sadler.*   Forcer, the son, had a liberal education ; and upon leaving Oxford, was entered of Gray's Inn ; and afterwards called by that Honourable Society to the Bar, where, for a short period, he practised as a pleader.   A sketch of his character is given below, from the pen of William Garbott, a poet whose numbers, partaking of ungarnished prose, may fitly be received as historical, notwithstanding their prolixity.   Garbott, after meandering with the subject of his lay, the New River, from its source past airy Newington, describes the Musick-house, gardens, and amusements, in the following lines :

> " Thro' Islington then glides my best lov'd theme,
> And Miles's Garden washes with his stream :
> Now F——r's garden is its proper name,
> Tho' Miles the man was, who first got it fame ;
> And tho' it's own'd Miles first did make it known,
> F——r improves the same, we all must own :

* " After the decease of Mr. Sadler, (says Sir John Hawkins) one Frances Forcer, a musician, and the composer of many Songs, printed in the Theatre of Musick, published by Henry Playford and John Carr in the years 1685, 1686, and 1687, became the occupier of the Wells and Musick-house.   His successor therein was a son of his, who had been bred up to the Law, and as some said, a Barrister ; he was the first that exhibited there the diversions of rope-dancing, tumbling, &c.   He was a very gentlemanly man, remarkably tall and athletick, and died in an advanced age, about the year 1730 (a misprint for 1740), at the Wells, which for many years had been the place of his residence."—*History of Musick*, vol. IV. p. 380.   Miles might succeed the elder Forcer.

There you may sit under the shady trees,
And drink and smoak, fann'd by a gentle breeze,
Behold the fish how wantonly they play,
And catch them also, if you please, you may—
Two noble swans swim by this garden side,
Of Water-fowl the glory and the pride,
Which to the Garden no small beauty are;
Were they but *black*, they would be much more rare;
With Ducks so tame, that from your hand they'll feed,
And, I believe, for that they sometimes bleed.
A noble Walk likewise adorns the place,
To which the River adds a greater grace:
There you may sit, or walk, do which you please,
Which best you like, and suits most with your ease.—
Now to the *Show-room* let's awhile repair,
To see the active feats performed there;
How the bold Dutch-man on the rope doth bound,
With greater air than others on the ground;
What capers does he cut! how backward leaps!
With Andrew Merry eyeing all his steps:
His comick humours with delight you see,
Pleasing unto the best of company.
The great *D'Aumont* has been diverting there, ⎫
With divers others of like character; ⎬
As by their gen'rous guifts they made appear. ⎭
The famous Tumbler lately is come o'er,
Who was the wonder of the other shore:
France, Spain, and Holland, and High-Germany,
Sweden, and Denmark, and fam'd Italy,
His active feats did with amazement see,
Which done by Man they thought could never be:
Amongst the rest, he falleth from on high,
Head foremost from the upper gallery,
And in his fall performs a Somerset,
The women shriek, in dread he'll break his neck,
And gently on his feet comes to the ground,
To the amazement of beholders round—

P

> Black Scaramouch, and Harlequin of fame,
> The Ladder-dance with forty I could name,
> Full as diverting, and of later date,
> You may see there, at a much cheaper rate
> Than at THE HOUSE, as well performed too ;
> You only pay for liquors, not the Show ;
> Such as neat Brandy, Southam Cyder fine,
> And grape's true juice as e'er was press'd from Vine."

Francis Forcer continued *lessee* of the premises until the time of his death, which happened April 1743. He directed, by his Will, that the lease of the house he then lived in, called or known by the name of Sadler's Wells, together with the scenery, implements, stock, furniture, household stuff and things thereunto belonging, should be sold, for the purpose of paying his specialty and other debts*. That direction was carried into effect soon after his decease : an event which probably served to strengthen the hopes of the

---

* The " New River, a poem, by William Garbott," was printed in 8vo. by " voluntary subscription." It is without date, and appears to have been published about 1720—30. He says,

> " All things conspire to please the best they can,
> Walks, waiters, river, liquor, and the MAN.
> Who would not go where pleasure doth invite ?
> Walks shady, silver stream, the eye's delight ;
> Ducks feeding from your hand, and snow-white swan,
> Balsamic Ale, and most obliging *man ;*
> So good it is, it's prais'd by all men's tongues,
> Healing as Balm of Gilead to the lungs.
> Miles in his way obliging was, we know,
> Yet F——r's language doth the softer flow ;
> Behav'our far genteeler of the two,
> By birth a Gentleman and breeding too :
> Oxford, for lib'ral Arts that is so fam'd,
> (Inferiour all, none equal can be nam'd)
> His Alma Mater was, it is well known,
> And Grey's Inn learned gave to him the gown.

Proprietors of a rival exhibition then open near the London Spaw, Clerkenwell*.

There is a View of old Sadler's Wells in a 4to Volume of Songs, engraved with Musick and incidental designs, as head-pieces; of which a copy is in my possession. It is called " Universal Harmony, or the Gentleman and Ladies Social Companion," and was published periodically during 1745 and 1746. At the exterior of the premises towards the head of the river stood a wall, where the iron rails are now fixed, and near to the river was a gate, inscribed, under a pediment, *Sadler's Wells*. The building on the Southern aspect had, in the first story, seven windows, four of them with antient casements, and three having modern sashes; the last were, probably, an addition made to the Musick-house by Forcer, for the purpose of habitation; and at one of the windows a single female, looking out, seems to confirm that conjecture. Of the basement story, an indistinctness of the engraving, and the height of the wall, makes it uncertain whether there were seven windows or only six, and that the Eastern end of the building, supported by pillars, formed a piazza. The well-house might have been a smaller build-

> Called he was from thence unto the Bar,
> And pleaded likewise as a Barrister.
> Another *Bar* he uses now, we know;
> Where most is got, the Counsel there will go :
> Altho' his fees may not so large be there,
> Greater the number of his clients are,
> Which makes the gain to be the greater far.
> He's judge, he's jury, and sole pleader there,
> A thing that is unknown at Westminster.
> Invested with this pow'r, not insolent,
> But unto ev'ry one he gives content."

* Francis Forcer, some years hefore he died, purchased a freehold piece of waste ground, forming part of what was called Mile-end Green, and including the rise of earth, lately well-known as Whitechapel Mount. It was charged with a large incumbrance, and the City of London had a long lease of it at £72, per annum. He had also a Copyhold estate at Ealing. The Freehold he gave to Catherine Forcer, his widow and executrix, for life; and the bulk of his property to Frances Forcer, his daughter by a former marriage, and to her heirs for ever.

ing, which appears detached, and standing near where the entrance-gates from the field are now erected. In the fore-ground the New River is introduced with a couple of Swans. An invitation to the Reader is given in

A New Song on Sadler's Wells; set by Mr. Brett.

" At eve when Silvan's shady scene
Is clad with spreading branches green,
And vary'd sweets all round display'd,
To grace the pleasant flow'ry meads,
Then those who are willing joys to taste
Where pleasures flow, and blessings last,
And God of Health in transport dwells,
Must all repair to Sadler's Wells.

There pleasant streams of Middleton
In gentle murmurs glide along;
In which the sporting fishes play,
To close each weary'd Summer's day:
And Musick's charms in lulling sounds
Of mirth and harmony abounds;
While nymphs and swains, with beaus and belles,
All praise the joys of Sadler's Wells.

The herds around o'er herbage green,
And bleating flocks, are sporting seen;
While Phœbus with its brightest rays,
The fertile soil doth seem to praise:
And Zephyrs with their gentlest gales,
Breathing more sweets than flow'ry vales;
Which give new health, and heat repells:
Such are the joys of Sadler's Wells."

The next Proprietor whose name has been preserved was Rosoman, an eminent builder, who in 1765 pulled down the old wooden building, and erected the Theatre on an enlarged scale in its present form, at the expence, as it is said, of L.4225. In fitting up the interior every attention was paid to the accommodating the audience with liquor during the performance, and for that purpose the seats had backs with ledged shelves at the top so as to secure the bottles for each row of visitors in succession ; and the glasses, having only short stems, were turned down over the mouth of the bottles. The terms upon which this objectionable trait of the old Theatre was continued and served out to the publick, are thus expressed in a Bill of 1773 : " Ticket for the boxes 3*s.* which will entitle the bearer to a pint of Port, Mountain, Lisbon, or Punch. Ticket for the pit 1*s.* 6*d.* Ticket for the gallery 1*s.* either of which, with an additional sixpence, will entitle the bearer to a pint of either of the aforesaid liquors. Any person choosing a second pint, may have it at 1*s.* the price paid at every other public place*." At benefits, the performers usually relied on their own popularity to fill the house; and announced, " boxes 3*s.* pit and gallery 1*s.* 6*d.* Those who chuse wine may have it at 2*s.* a bottle†."

---

* There was a temporary revival of this custom during the Seasons of 1803, 4, and 5 ; and the wine supplied at 2*s.* the bottle, and 1*s.* the pint.

† The three following Advertisements are given from the London Daily Post of Saturday, July 3, 1742 :

" NEW WELLS. At the New Wells, near the London-Spaw, Clerkenwell, this Evening will be presented several new exercises of rope-dancing by Madame Brila, Mademoiselle Brila, lately arrived from Paris, and the two Miss Rayners. With singing by Mr. Johnson, and Mrs. Hill. And a variety of new dances (both serious and comic) by Mons. Granier, the two Masters and Miss Granier, Mr. Miles, Mr. Clacket, the two Miss Scotts, Miss Rayner, and others. Also a Hornpipe by Mr. Jones from Bath, who plays on the violin at the same time. Also Mons. Brila, the famous Equilibrist, will perform several new balances, different to what he performed at Goodman's-fields the last season. And Mons. Brila's son, aged three years, performs on the stiff rope, and several curiosities of balancing with his father. The whole to conclude with two views of the Amphitheatre, in Ranelagh Gardens at Chelsea. To begin every evening at five o'clock."

" SADLER's-WELLS. At Sadler's Wells, adjoining to the New-River Head, Islington, this evening at five o'Clock, will begin the usual diversions. Consisting of rope-dancing by Madem. Kerman, Mr. Bodin, just arrived from Holland, and others. Tumbling by Mons. Dominique, Mr. Kerman, Mr. Bodin, Mr. Williams, and others ; singing by Mr. Hemskirk and Mr. Brett ; variety of dances (both serious and comic) by Mons. Dumont, Mons. Baudouin, Mr. Daven-

In 1778 the whole of the inside of the House was taken down and materially improved.   The cieling was raised considerably, which afforded an
opportunity of making the boxes and back of the pit, &c. more lofty ; whereby the spectator not only enjoyed a freer air, but also commanded at every
part of the House a view of the whole extent of the stage.   The Theatre
also acquired a degree of beauty from the neatness of its shape and the sim-
plicity of its ornaments.

port, Mr. Osbeldiston, Mr. Rayner, Mrs. Bullock, Mrs. La Font, Mrs. Rayner, Mrs. Phillips,
Miss Story, Master Matthews, and Miss Wright.   With several extraordinary performances
by M. Henderick Kerman, the famous ladder-dancer."

"GOODMAN'S-FIELDS.   At the New Wells, the bottom of Lemon-street, Goodman's fields,
this evening will be perform'd several new exercises of rope-dancing, tumbling, vaulting, and
equilibres.   Rope-dancing by Mons. Magito, Mons. Janno ; and Madem. de Lisle will perform several exercises on the slack rope.   And variety of tumbling by the celebrated Mr.
Towers, the English tumbler, Mons. Guitar, Mons. Janno, and Mr. Hough.   Singing by Miss
Karver, and dancing (both serious and comic) by Mr. Carney, Mr. Shawford, Madem. Renos,
Madem. Duval, and Mrs. Hough.   With several new equilibres by the famous Little Russia
Boy, who performs several ballances upon the top of a ladder eight foot high ; and then comes
down, head foremost, through the rounds of the ladder ; he also performs all the balances on
the chairs, and several others never yet perform'd, which no one can do in England but him-
self.   To which will be added, a great scene after the manner of the Ridotto al' Fresco.   The
whole to conclude with a grand representation of Water Works, as in the Doge's Gardens at
Venice.   The scenes, cloaths, and musick, all new.   The scenes painted by Mons. Deroto.
To begin every evening exactly at half an hour after five."

The situation of the New Wells near the London Spaw, is shown by a public-house still
retaining the sign of the London Spaw, which has a front towards Spa-fields, forming the corner house of Rosamon's-row, Clerkenwell, and was formerly the place where the water was
obtained.   The New Wells belonged to Rosamon, before he obtained the possession of Sadler's
Wells ; and the site of the building, as I am informed, was about No. 4 and 5 of the street
now called by his name.   If the supplying liquor to the audience was not adopted at this place,
it explains the allusion made by Garbott, in the lines above-quoted, as to the amusement at
Sadler's Wells being cheaper than at THE HOUSE.   At what period the New Wells was first
opened, or when finally closed, I have not discovered.

The New Wells, Goodman's fields, were situate in and gave name to Well-yard, Lemon-
street.   Prelluer was one of the composers for this Theatre, and published the Musick of Bau-

About the same period, if not some years earlier, the elder Dibdin composed several favourite pieces for this Theatre, and a niche was not unfrequently occupied in the daily papers with " Intelligence from Sadler's Wells." The musick was popular, the dances were novel, and the pantomines celebrated for their comic tricks and changes; in which character they were admirably supported by the late " truly excellent master of dumb-shew, Signor Grimaldi ;" whose genius and humour seem to be held through heritage by his descendant, the present representative of similar characters.

" From Rosoman, Sadler's Wells went to the celebrated and admired veteran performer, late of Drury-lane Theatre, Mr. King ; Serjeant, the trumpeter ; and Arnold, a goldsmith and jeweller ; from whom Mr. Arnold, and Mr. Wroughton, now of Drury Lane, purchased it for L.12,000. The Wells afterwards became the joint property of Messrs. Wroughton ; Mr. Siddons, husband of the greatly-valued tragic actress ; Mr. Hughes, proprietor of several provincial theatres ; Mr. Coates, a linen-draper ; and Mr. Arnold, jun. And lastly, in 1802, it was purchased by Mr. Charles Dibdin, jun. ; Mr. T. Dibdin, his brother, author of the Cabinet, &c. ; Mr. Reeve the com-

cis and Philemon, a burletta, performed there about the time of the Rebellion. Some songs with Musick, are also in print that were sung there, and prove that it shared no inconsiderable portion of public favour. More than thirty years ago, the Theatre formed an angle of some Tobacco warehouses of subsequent erection, and the Coopers were in the custom of showing it to persons having business there, as at that time part of the stage and boxes remained in a mutilated state. Those persons working at the warehouses, as well as others residing in the neighbourhood, commonly described the Company performing there as Sadler's Company, and that either he or his successor removed to Islington, and carried from thence the designation of " Sadler's Wells." This erroneous conjecture was probably founded on the same company performing at both theatres.

The above Theatres, together with Hallam's Theatre in May Fair, and two Gaming houses in Govent Garden, were all presented by the Grand Jury of Middlesex in May 1744, as " places kept apart for the encouragement of luxury, extravagance, idleness, and other wicked illegal purposes."—*Noorthouchs History of London*, 1773, *p.* 350. See Gent. Mag. vol. XIV. p. 278.

poser ; Mr. Andrewes, many years the very excellent scene-painter to this Theatre ; and two Gentlemen in the City."*

Upon the 2d of April 1804, being Easter Monday, and the usual period for the Season commencing at this Theatre, there was produced a variation of the usual entertainments, under the title of *Naumachia.* It consists of an incidental scene upon real water, and the first representation was the Siege of Gibraltar. This grand and singular introduction of the aquatic element, upon so large a scale, within the walls of a theatre, is from necessity limited to the concluding scene, and effected by removing the whole flooring of the stage, which is over a large bason of water ; and whereon have been seen floating boats, ships, and sea monsters, of a size exceeding all the tin and paste-board illusions of the Patent Theatres. The proximity of the New River enabled the proprietors to plan and complete this novel and popular exhibition.

The present Theatre consists of a single range of boxes, with a pit and gallery ; and the price of admission are 4*s.* 2*s.* and 1*s.* The performances usually consist of a light comic dance, a serious ballet, a short pantomine, occasionally rope-dancing, and a grand historical spectacle. A few seasons past there was the appropriate motto over the stage of " Mirth, admit me of thy crew ;" afterwards drop boards were used instead of the motto, to communicate the title of each successive piece, and which plan was similar to one of the most antient usages of the English stage, that of nailing upon a pole near the centre of the stage, the title of the piece acted, as will be shown hereafter. The performances commence soon after six o'clock, and end about eleven o'clock.

To conclude ; it is but justice to the established respectability of this Theatre, to observe the tippling lure above noticed as formerly affixed to the Bills, is no longer continued ; and the public have crowded† the house repeatedly through several seasons, although the wine is changed into water. Neither

---

* Malcolm's Londinium Redivivum, vol, III. p. 233.

† The melancholy accident whereby 18 persons were killed, and several others hurt severely, upon a crowded night in 1807 is fully detailed in the Gentleman's Magazine, vol. LXXVII. p. 971.

should it be omitted to be noticed that this is almost the only Theatre within the circle of the Metropolis, that can be mentioned as having the lobbies, those lounging-places of vice, free from the disgusting and constant display of folly and shameless prostitution.

DORSET GARDENS THEATRE.—Since the account of this Theatre appeared, (*vide* p. 91,) I have met with " *The Young Gallant's Academy, or, Directions how he should behave in all Places aad Company, by Sam. Overcome*, 1674 ;" again reprinted as " *by S. V.* 1696." This little octavo volume was a slight alteration of " Decker's Gull's Horn-book," (a circumstance the Editor of the late valuable edition of that amusing work does not appear to have been acquainted with) and the characters and places re-adapted to the times. The scene of the Theatre is therefore altered from the Globe ; and Chap. 5. concludes, " Some are gone to one theatre, some to the other. Let us take a pair of oars for Dorset-stairs, and so into the Theatre after them as fast as we can." With other alterations of the original, the following is given as instructions : " The play-house is free for entertainment, allowing room as well to the Farmer's son as to a Templer ; yet it is not fit that, he whom the most Taylor's bills make room for when he comes, should be basely, like a viol, cased up in a corner : therefore, I say, let our gallant, (having paid his *half crown* and given the door-keeper his *ticket*) presently advance himself into the middle of the *pit*, where hauing made his honour to the rest of the Company, but especially to the Vizard-masks, let him pull out his comb, and manage his flaxen wig with all the grace he can. Hauing so done, the next step is to give a hum to the China orange-wench, and give her her own rate for her oranges (for 'tis below a gentleman to stand haggling like a Citizen's wife) and then to present the fairest to the next Vizard-mask. And that I may encourage our Gallant not like Tradesman to save a shilling, and so sit but in the middle gallery, let him but consider what large comings-in are pursed up sitting in the pit.—First, a conspicuous eminence is gotten, by which means the best and most essential parts of a gentleman, as his fine cloaths and perruke are perfectly revealed.—Second,

Q

by sitting in the pit, if you be a knight, you may happily get you a mistress;
which, if you would, I advise you never to be absent when Epsome Wells is
plaid : for,

> We see the Wells have stoln the Vizard-masks away."

There may also be added the following further particulars of the final
destruction of this Theatre.

In the Spring of 1703, a general repair of the building for the purpose
of re-opening having commenced, the Grand Jury of London, at the July
Sessions held at the Old Bailey, by their presentment stated there was something yet wanting towards carrying on the new reformation of manners ;
and therefore they humbly proposed the following matter for the consideration of the Court, which may be given in their own words : viz. " The having some effectual course taken (if possible) to prevent the youth of this city
from resorting to the play-houses, which we rather mention because the
play-house bills are again posted up throughout the city, in contempt of a
former presentment and a positive order of the Lord Mayor and Court of
Aldermen to the contrary ;* as also because we are informed that a play-
house within the liberties of this city, which has been of late disused and
neglected, is at this time refitting in order to be used as formerly. We do
not presume to prescribe to this honourable Court, but we cannot question,
but that, if they shall think fit, humbly to address her Majesty in this case,
she will be graciously pleased to prevent it."

This measure was echoed by the fastidious canting author of the Observator, as a " very good presentment against the play-houses, particularly
against one of them now fitting up in Dorset Gardens."†

The expected opposition of the Citizens, or, perhaps, some order from the
Master of the Revels, occasioned the plan for re-opening this Theatre to be

---

* In June 1700, there was an order made by the Lord Mayor and Court of Aldermen,
forbidding to affix in any part of the city or the liberties thereof the Play-house bills, according to the presentment of the Grand Jury at the last sessions at the Old Bailey.

Postman, June 25, 1700.

† See *Observator,* July 14—17, 1703, and the consistent reply to the same in *Heraclitus
Ridens,* No. 1. August 1, 1703.

abandoned; and I have not yet discovered that any diversion was afterwards exhibited. In 1709 it was razed to the ground; as appears by the following extract from a periodical paper, called *The Gazette à-la-mode: or Tom Brown's Ghost*, No. 3. Thursday, May 26, 1709.

" I wonder (says the Writer) that a man whose wits run so much a wool gathering as my Coz. *Bickerstaff's* should not all this time have pick'd up some Epigram, Elegy, or other doleful ditty, on such a lamentable occasion as the pulling down the Theatre in Dorset-Garden; upon which melancholy subject, an old acquaintance of my friend *Isaac's*, a water-poet, has been so kind as to oblige me with the following lines, composed and dated on board the *Folly*, now lying opposite the ruined Play-house.

" Ye Muses weep, weep all ye Nine,
The Poets vainly call Divine:
See there that scene of Melancholy
While yet here floats the sinking Folly;
From whence that falling pile we view,
Once sacred to the Gods and you,
Which buskin'd Heroes use to tread,
And represent the glorious dead.
Now, now, alas, 'tis servile made,
And is from pleasure turn'd to trade.
The manag'd stage, and well-wrought scene
Adorn'd with exquisite machine,
No longer please our wand'ring eyes,
They once engag'd with such surprise;
When there we saw a dying part,
Play'd to the life by Moh'n or Hart.
Here grieve yourselves in tears away,
And put on Cypress 'stead of Bay;
While laurels crown your sons no more,
That dare thus rudely 'front your pow'r.
No more shine on the stage with grace
That is profan'd with every ass:
Heroes of old neglected sleep,
And in their peaceful ashes weep,
That us'd each night within this place
To show the grandure of their race,

And prove the justness of their life and doom
Whether perform'd in Greece or Rome.
Mysterious Œdipus appears
Here full of grief as he's of years;
Young Ammon's passion mounts as high, ⎫
As it in Babylons cou'd fly, ⎬
And Clytus cou'd not nobler die. ⎭
Here Scipio conquers, and Hannibal
At Canna cou'd not greater fall.
Cæsar himself receiv'd his fate ⎫
Not with more majesty and state ⎬
Than Hart cou'd represent the great: ⎭
Brutus and Cassius were outdone
Themselves by Betterton and Moh'n.
And shall that pile dwindle to wood,
Where once such mighty Heroes stood? *
Shall burlesque Theatres arise,
To entertain poor vulgar eyes;
And Dorset's once fam'd glories sink,
Without a deluge of poetic ink.
Tell it no more, no more complain,
Since all your sorrows are in vain.
The fabrick now in ruin lies
That once ascended to the skies,
And that which once such pleasure gave,
Is now prepar'd to be your grave. " †

The site was used as a timber-yard for several years. It is described as such in some lines " On a Lady's favourite Cat," inserted in " *Count Piper's Packet, being a choice and curious Collection of Manuscript papers in prose and verse*, 1732.

" Near that fam'd place, where in old times there stood
A Theatre; but now huge piles of wood:
Where silver Thames runs gliding for the stairs,
And Watermen stand bawling to their fares;

* Now made a Wood yard.   † A Saw-pit.

Where noble Dorset claims a royalty.
And Bride's fair steeple towers to the sky ;
Where mug-house members kept their clubs of late,
And rioters met their untimely fate :
Close in a nook a little house you'll find," &c.

A South view of the Dorset Gardens Theatre is given in the Gentleman's Magazine for July 1814. Some alteration was made in the exterior of the building, after the view was taken that is given in Settle's *Empress of Morocco*, unless that represents, as probable, the North front. At the time of the repairing above noticed, the arms and ornaments might be altered, as the view from which the above-mentioned engraving is copied, is supposed to have been made after the repairs were completed. Other views, in the same direction, may be found in the large sheet maps of " *A Prospect of London and Westminster, taken at several stations to the Southward thereof, by William Morgan ;*" and also in " Henry Overton's *New Prospect of London of the South side, &c.*" dedicated to Gideon Harvey by the publisher Jas. Walker. It stood near the mouth of Fleet ditch, which had on the opposite side a handsome structure, with a balcony, belonging to a noted empiric, Dr. Salmon ; a part of which is shewn in the view.

In Buck's views (1749) the site is represented as a Timber yard.

CHINA-HALL, ROTHERHITHE.—This suburban Theatre is supposed to have been opened in the summer of 1777. It was formed from the warehouse of a paper-manufacturer; and novelty crowning the first season with sufficient encouragement, the proprietors ventured to embellish and materially improve the premises : the advertisement for the commencement of the following season, stating the Proprietors " have spared no expence in enlarging and beautifying the Theatre ; and as they are determined to preserve the exactest punctuality in the time of beginning, and to make regularity and decorum their chief study, hope they shall render themselves deserving of that favourable encouragement they have before experienced." The prices of admission were, boxes, 3s. pit, 2s. gallery, 1s. and time of commencing varied by the season from half-past six to seven o'clock. The Wonder and

Lying Valet; Love in a Village with Comical Courtship (a new piece) were among the pieces performed; and in the season of 1778 one of the performers, was the late celebrated George Frederick Cooke. Some time in the winter of 1778-9 the whole building was destroyed by fire.

RUCKHOLT-HOUSE, LEYTON, ESSEX.—Ruckholt-house is said to have been once the mansion of Queen Elizabeth; and is now mentioned as forming, for a short period, an auxiliary place of amusement for the Summer to the established Theatres, and situate within the environs of London. It was opened about the year 1742 by the proprietor, Wm. Barton, with public breakfasts, weekly concerts, and occasional oratorios. The place is thus described in a ballad addressed

To DELIA,

An Invitation to Ruckholt-house.

" Delia, in whose form we trace
All that can a virgin grace,
Hark where pleasure blith as May,
Bids us to Rockholt [haste] away.

Verdant vestos, melting sounds,
Magic echoes, fairy rounds,
Beauties ev'ry where surprize.
Sure that spot dropt from the skies.
Delia, in, &c.*

---

* The following votive ditty upon Hampstead, and the Wells, I have only discovered since the note at page 104 was printed; and which is not mentioned, I believe, by the intelligent Author of the recent valuable Volume upon " *The Topography and Natural History of Hampstead."* It may be found in " *The Musical Entertainer, engraved by George Bickham, Jun.* fol. II. No. 15," entituled " The Beautys of Hampstead," and also as a broad-side, from which the present copy is taken.

" Summer's heat the town invades,
All repair to cooling shades,
  How inviting,
  How delighting,
Are the hills, and flow'ry meads !

Here, where lovely Hampstead stands,
And the neighb'ring vale commands,
  What surprising
  Prospects rising,
All around adorn the lands.

Here ever woody mounts arise,
There verdant lawns delight our eyes,
  Where Thames wanders,
  In meanders,
Lofty domes approach the skies.

Here are grottos, purling streams,
Shades defying Titan's beams,
  Rosy bowers,
  Fragrant flowers,
Lovers wishes, Poets themes.

Of the chrystal bubbling well,
Life, and strength, the current swell,
  Health and pleasure,
  (Heav'nly treasure !)
Smiling here, united dwell.

Here, nymphs and swains indulge your hearts,
Share the joys our scene imparts,
  Here be strangers
  To all dangers,
All—but those of Cupid's darts."

The " sweet singers of Ruckholt" are immortalized by Shenstone ; and the place appears to have been the drive of fashion for about three seasons. In " *Music in good time, a new ballad,* 1745," fol. it is enumerated with other places in the following stanzas :

> " Oh L—c—n, oh C——ke, and each belman appear
> With your songs and your sonnets to charm ev'ry ear ;
> To spin catches and odes, and your past'rals fine,
> Assist them *Grub Phœbus,* assist bunters nine.
> > Derry down, &c.

> That *Vauxhall* and *Ruckholt* and *Ranelagh* too,
> And *Hoxton* and *Sadler's,* both old and new,
> My Lord *Cobham's* head, and the *Dulwich* Green-man,
> May make as much pastime as ever they can.
> > Derry down, &c.

It is uncertain whether public amusements continued after the Summer of 1746. The House was pulled down about 1757.

LILLIPUTIAN THEATRE, WHITECHAPLE.—The premises had been altered from the Angel and Crown Tavern, and opened as a Theatre about the month of October 1778, with the price of admission to the boxes 3s. pit 2s. Among the pieces represented were Midas, Harlequin's Revels, Love in a Village, with new scenery, &c.*

---

* A correspondent of the Gentleman's Magazine, Vol. LXXXIII. p. 656, remarks, that the word " revolution" which occurs at the commencement of the remarks on Sadler's Wells, was undoubtedly intended for " restoration"—the amendment is evidently correct, although some of Haslewood's enemies might affirm that he did not know the difference between the two events.—The well-known *Music House* was established by Richard, more familiarly called *Dick* Sadler.

V

NOTICES RELATIVE TO THE ROXBURGHE CLUB.

I. ANNIVERSARY OF THE BIBLIOMANIO-ROXBURGHE CLUB.*

July 10, 1813.

MR. URBAN,—

AMONGST the important events of later times, there are few that have excited a greater degree of interest than the transactions which took place at ROXBURGHE-HOUSE in July 1812. The warfare in St. James's Square was equalled only by the courage and gallantry displayed on the plains of Salamanca about the same period; and history will doubtless relate these celebrated feats in the same volume, for the information and astonishment of posterity. As a pillar, or other similar memorial, could not be conveniently erected to mark the spot where so many *bibliographical champions* fought and conquered, another method was adopted, to record their fame, and to perpetuate this brilliant epoch in literary annals. Accordingly, a phalanx of the most hardy veterans has been enrolled, under the banner of the far-famed Valdarfer's Boccacio of 1471, bearing the title of the ROXBURGHE-CLUB. As their proceedings are too momentous to perish with the fleeting page of a newspaper, Mr. Urban is requested to inscribe them on the adamantine columns of the Gentleman's Magazine.

The first Anniversary meeting of this noble band, was celebrated at the St. Alban's Tavern, on Thursday the 17th ult., being the memorable day on which the before-named Boccacio was sold for £2260. The chair was taken by Earl Spencer, (perpetual President of the Club), supported by

---

* From the Gentleman's Magazine for July 1813.

R

Lords Morpeth and Gower, and the following gentlemen,* viz., Sir E. Brydges, Messrs W. Bentham, W. Bolland, J. Dent, J. F. Dibdin, (Vice-President), Francis Freeling, Henry Freeling, Jos. Haslewood, Rich. Heber, Thos. C. Heber, G. Isted, R. Lang, J. H. Markland, J. D. Phelps, T. Ponton, jun., J. Townley, E. V. Utterson, and R. Wilbraham. Upon the cloth being removed, the following appropriate toasts were delivered from the chair :—

1. The cause of Bibliomania all over the world.
2. The immortal memory of Christopher Valdarfer, printer of the Boccacio of 1471.
3. The immortal memory of William Caxton, first English printer.
4. The immortal memory of Wynkyn de Worde.
5. The immortal memory of Richard Pynson.
6. The immortal memory of Julian Notary.
7. The immortal memory of William Faques.
8. The immortal memory of the Aldine family.
9. The immortal memory of the Stephenses.
10. The immortal memory of John Duke of Roxburghe.

After these, the health of the noble President was proposed, and received by the company standing, with three times three. Then followed the health of the worthy Vice-President, (proposed by Mr. Heber), which it is scarcely necessary to observe, was drunk with similar honours ; for the name of Dibdin (the De Bure of the 19th century,) is as highly prized amongst the lovers of 𝔅𝔩𝔞𝔠𝔨 𝔏𝔢𝔱𝔱𝔢𝔯 lore, as that of Nelson by the valorous sons of Neptune.

The President was succeeded in the chair by Lord Gower ; who, at midnight, yelded it to Mr. Dent ; and that gentleman gave way to the prince of Bibliomaniacs, Mr. Heber. Though the night, or rather the morning,

* Amongst the absentees were His Grace the Duke of Devonshire, who was prevented attending the Anniversary by indisposition, the Marquis of Blandford, and Sir M. M. Sykes, Bart.

wore apace, it was not likely that a seat so occupied would be speedily deserted; accordingly, the "regal purple stream" ceased not to flow, till "morning ope'd her golden gates," or, in plain terms, till past 4 o'clock.

The Roxburghe Club is limited in number to THIRTY-ONE members, and one black ball is fatal to the candidate who offers himself upon a vacancy; so that a Directorship of the India Board, or of the Bank of England, will henceforth be a situation of comparative insignificance. Amongst other Statutes enacted by this body, there is one of too important a nature to be passed over in silence; upon every successive anniversary, one of the members is to produce a reprint of a scarce and curious tract, or to print some original manuscripts, and the number of copies printed will be confined to that of the Club. The merit of this happily-conceived law, is due to HORTENSIUS,* who, in the most spirited manner, offered to put it in force, by a reprint of Lord Surrey's Virgil; with a margin of such proportionate elegance as might cause his favourite Michel Le Noir (were he living) to die with envy and dispair. In future, no child can be said to be portionless whose father is a ROXBURGHIAN, as *one* of these gems will doubtless prove an ample provision!

I have now, Mr. Urban, performed my object, in furnishing you with some account of this glorious day; and you will readily admit, that when the origin of this Institution, and the vast and interesting schemes which it embraces, are well considered, The ROXBURGHE CLUB must be regarded, in a national point of view, as conferring dignity and importance upon the land that gave it birth.

With my hearty wishes for the success of our first toast, in which you will cordially join, " The Cause of BIBLIOMANIA all over the World,"

I am,

Sir,

Your's, &c.

TEMPLARIUS.

* Mr. Baron Bolland.—*Vide* Dibdin's Bibliomania, p. 176.

2. Observations on the Proceedings of the Roxburghe Club.*

S——, *Aug.* 7, 1813.

Mr. Urban,—

The occurrences at the Roxburghe Sale (in July 1812.) have indeed, as Templarius observes in your last number, excited no trifling degree of interest in the literary world; but the society which has been formed in consequence of these occurrences, and the proceedings adopted by the members of that society, appear to call for still more attention. The honourable members of the Roxburghe Club, have, no doubt, persuaded themselves that they are aiding the diffusions of useful knowledge, and promoting the interests of Literature. But, instead of diffusing knowledge, they selfishly cut off the springs which should feed it; and, instead of promoting the interests of Literature, they materially injure them.

For if selfishness may be defined to be, " *that affection of the mind, by which a man is impelled to study his own advantage, without any regard, or even in opposition, to that of others;*" selfishness must be the most appropriate term whereby to designate the proceedings of a body of men, who have determined annually to print or reprint some valuable or scarce work, but to confine the number of copies to be printed to the number of their Club, which is already limited to THIRTY-ONE: thereby depriving the whole literary world (with the exception of only thirty-one persons) of all the information and entertainment which might be derived from the perusal of these scarce and valuable works. That they have a right, or, in other words, that it is lawful for them to do so, cannot be disputed; but it is doubtless selfish, and by no means becoming men who have any pretensions to Literature, and is so far from tending to diffuse knowledge, that it can serve only to confine and repress it.

* From the Gentleman's Magazine for September 1813.

And that they materially injure the cause of Literature is evident: for while they, anxious that those works which are already too scarce, may not become less so, have resolved to print only a very limited number of copies, the idea has been seized with avidity by some publishers; who, when announcing to the world the publication of some valuable work, in order to keep up its price, and prevent its falling into the hands of too many who might be disposed to look into it, at the same time advertise that only a certain number of copies will be printed.* I am not prepared to assert that this idea might not, of itself, have entered the minds of the publishers ; but the example of men of such distinction as the members of the Roxburghe Club, certainly affords a precedent of no little weight, and may be referred to by them with the greatest exultation.

Being myself one of the many who take delight in literary pursuits, I cannot, unmoved, observe proceedings, which, from their outset, throw obstacles in the way of almost all who desire to prosecute those studies, which, under any circumstance of life, can afford so much real comfort and genuine satisfaction. That the members of the Roxburghe Club are at present any thing but patrons and supporters of Literature, is, I think, very evident: but I confidently look forward to the time, and that not far distant, when the members of this body will shew themselves really anxious to promote the diffusion of knowledge, and serve the true interests of literature, not by merely bearing the name of *Bibliomaniacs*, but by allowing the world to enjoy, together with them, the benefit of works at present scarce, and difficult to be procured, and by putting it in the power of men of moderate income to obtain a portion of that science and information, which " Nihilominus" ipsis lucebit, " cum" illis " accenderint."

Yours, &c.

J. M.**

---

* This practice is as old as the time of Tom Hearne [if not older] who never usually printed more copies of any of his Valuable Works than were subscribed for. If we recollect right of his Edition of the Acts of the Apostles, only a Hundred Copies were thrown off.

3. THE UTILITY OF LITERARY ASSOCIATIONS DEMONSTRATED.*

Oct. 9, 1813.

MR. URBAN,—

I CANNOT coincide in opinion with your correspondent J. M.** that the zeal of the Roxburghe Club is mis-directed, or that their labours are un-friendly to Literature.

That they are, on the contrary, highly beneficial, will appear from the following considerations :—

First, The fame of the unusually high prices which rare Articles in Literature have lately obtained, has excited an extraordinary diligence in the search after, and care in the preservation of, such articles : it has ope-rated favourably upon all books, by inducing the possessors to preserve what might otherwise have been destroyed, in hope that it would be found to possess considerable value. Within my recollection, and that of many others, Old Books, out of the common course of reading, found their way in large quantities to the cheesemongers; hence it is that copies of some works have become so rare, and that others are supposed to be extinct, be-cause references to them occur in different works, while the books them-selves are nowhere to be found. The revival of a literary taste amongst those who have spacious palaces in which to deposit such *ornamental, en-tertaining,* and *intellectual* furniture, and the means of recompensing persons who take upon themselves the labour of collecting, collating, &c. has already preserved much curious and valuable matter from destruction, and opposed something like a barrier to the future ravages of time and accident.

Secondly, The introduction of Literature amongst the amusements of the higher ranks of society makes it fashionable, and thus promotes useful exer-tions in the cause amongst the more numerous *imitators* of the great, *who form minor and subordinate libraries of rarities of the second class.*

* From the Gentleman's Magazine for October 1813.

Thirdly, If the members of the Roxburghe Club only add thirty-one, (which by the bye are not only copies but *fac-similes*), to the existing very small numbers of any scarce works, by depositing these copies in Libraries where they are preserved with due care, they sufficiently guard against the final extinction of those works; and while gentlemen allow their Collections to be seen and consulted by authors and other men of taste who wish it, there is, I conceive, not the least ground for complaint. Reprinting works (although only in very small impressions), by consuming materials and labour, promotes trade, and is so far a positive good. It is so much out of the revenues of Noblemen and Gentlemen of liberal mind and literary taste set apart and given to *Literature.* To grudge the Donors the gratification of possessing rarities is, in my opinion, puerile. " Never, " (says the proverb) " look a gift-horse in the mouth."

Those publishers who are charged with imitating the Bibliomaniacs in printing small numbers, stand in need of very little defence: in general they are much more sinned against than sinning. In a commercial country like this, the principles of trade, and habit of calculating the value of money, have sometimes had an unfavourable bearing upon those speculations which depend for success on public patronage. The work of merit once published, the *would-be-patron* indulges himself with a gratuitous sight at a bookseller's shop, or borrows for perusal or reference, and waits till, according to his *not very liberal calculation,* the *necessities* of the publisher shall oblige him to dispose of his books by *auction,* at one-half or one-third of their value. Out of such miscarriages arise the bankruptcy of publishers, the chagrin and poverty of authors; and, were the practice universal, would proceed also the absolute extinction of literary spirit. No injury, therefore, is done to these gentlemen, in making it at least probable that their *thrifty policy* will so far defeat itself, as that they may ultimately be obliged to pay a very *advanced price* for, or go without, the *interesting* and *instructive* volume with which they *some day* intend to grace their book-shelves; while it is *just* to the liberal and manly patrons, thus to secure to *his property* a *certain, fair,* and *improving* value.—In short, we have no law in England, at present, by which a man is compelled to buy expensive paper, and pay for printing it, and then sell it for little more than the price of waste ; and certainly there can be no *other* motive to such a practice.   The law, which compels every publisher to *give* to the extent of ELEVEN copies, is by *some* thought sufficiently *hard*.   But of this more anon.

Yours, &c.

A. C.

4. REMARKS ON THE OBSERVATIONS OF J. M.**

West-Smithfield, October 18, 1813.

MR. URBAN,—

THE feeling of surprise with which I read the remarks of your correspondent, (J. M.**) on the " Proceedings of the Roxburghe Club," has, I trust, also pervaded the minds of a large majority of your readers.   The charges against that respectable body, to which your candour has given a place in your valuable Miscellany, seem to call loudly for a complete defence of the Bibliomania, which I trust you have already received from a more able pen ; but that which is the business of every man, is for that very reason frequently neglected by all, and the supporter of the most erroneous opinions is too often left to triumph in the belief that what remains unanswered, is also irrefragable.

To contend merely for the harmlessness of the Institution in question, would be, in my mind, a culpable humiliation ; yet who can deny that it is at least inoffensive ? The utility of Associations, which bring together and promote good-fellowship amongst men of congenial sentiments and similar pursuits, has been too long acknowledged by the general suffrage of mankind to become now a matter of controversy ; but an establishment like that of the Roxburghe Club, formed for the ostensible purpose of giving dignity and honour to mental exertion, must, in my humble opinion, extend its beneficial effects beyond any possible calculation.

That the proceedings of a body of men thus united have originated in selfishness, is at least useless to assert, and as useless to deny ; take away this main-spring of human actions, and where is the stimulus to virtue of any kind, to liberality, or even to friendship itself ? Is there any dishonour

in confessing the formation of our natures, or any merit but in yielding up
our passions to the command of virtue? A couplet from Pope will decide
the matter;

> " Heav'n form'd a whole the whole to bless,
> And mutual wants breed mutual happiness."

If it be confessed that whim and fancy have a considerable influence with
the lovers of books, who is so ready as the Bibliomaniac to rally himself
upon his own foible, or to submit to the sarcasms of others when dictated
by good sense, and softened by good humour?

It appears to give your correspondent particular offence, that the number
of copies of those works re-printed by the Society, is not to exceed that of
the members composing the Club. The answer to this will be readily anticipated : if it exceed that number, where should it stop? or how could
benevolence the most Quixotic be extended to the gratification of every
one's wish? I mean only as to the absolute possession of the works in question ; for it is well known to be the great pleasure of every Collector to
throw open his *Literary Museum*, not merely to his private friends, but to
any intelligent inquirer who shall think it worth his while to make a becoming application.

That the Roxburghe Club should degrade themselves into a mere set of
partners in a literary traffick, who could for a moment desire? But are they
not the prompt and eager patrons of every literary undertaking which requires
their aid? Let the Booksellers who have, at this moment, various reprints in
the press, which they could not have so multiplied without the unrestrained
use of the rare originals, answer this question. That the number of such
impressions is uniformly small, is owing to that degree of selfishness in
man, which we may deplore, but cannot correct. What is common who
will covet? What is to be had at any time, who will fix the time for buy-
ing? Besides, I will maintain, that it is not essential to the interests of
Literature that every work, of every kind, should obtain a universal circulation ; but let the voice of the public declare what it is that will be really
acceptable, and I know of no obstacle to their gratification ; but it is not ne-

s

cessary for a Roxburghe Club to become the mimic of a society for distributing cheap and useful tracts.

The true lover of Literature can contemplate the possessions of others, if not with pleasure, at least without malignant envy ; in books there is almost an endless variety, and always a sufficiency within the reach of every man for the delightful recreation of the longest life. And for the occasional use of the treasures of others, I have never heard of a single instance in which it has been denied ; nay, it is even invited : witness the numerous Catalogues of private Libraries, printed for the chief purpose of affording facilities to those who would trace a curious article to its present possessor.

Yet your correspondent says, that " The Honourable Members, instead of diffusing knowledge, selfishly cut off the springs that should feed it ; and, instead of promoting the interests of Literature, they materially injure them." How, in the name of reason, can this accusation apply to men, who have determined, annually, to give to some curious relick of antient wisdom, a chance of descending to the latest posterity ?

The Noble Members of the Roxburghe Club are setting a most meritorious example to the world ; they have done, and are doing, all that can be wished of them. That every true Bibliomaniac will, in a degree, envy them the possession of their own productions, cannot be doubted ; but it is not in necessity, nor in the nature of the thing, that the number should be extended ; and if the charge of injury be not refuted, I will be jocular enough to say, that every lover of good eating and drinking will have an equal right to complain of his exclusion from the annual dinner.

I consider it, Mr. Urban, to constitute one of the brightest hopes of Britain, that the Bibliomania is spreading wide among her youth. Let the passion for books commence in foppery itself, (to use a term as harsh as peevishness could invent), and it will rarely fail to end in the most permanent advantage, and not more so to the individual, than to all with whom such an attachment shall connect him through life. In the present day, the acquisition of a Library, which shall be admired for the taste and judgment with which it is selected, forms a prominent feature in the pursuits even of men of fashion ; who formerly, upon being questioned as to their literary attainments, would, almost to a man, have answered with Sheridan's Moses, "*Nothing to do with books.*"

My object, Mr. Urban, is solely the establishment of truth upon a subject of no mean importance. I know not how it may strike others; but, for my own part, I am delighted at the thought, that, under the auspices of a combination which aims at nothing but the union of social pleasure with mental improvement, we may look with confidence for the time when no exertion of intellect shall want a patron, nor merit of any kind a friend. In a word, Mr. Urban, that the Roxburghe Club is a useful institution, and worthy the noblest spirits of a nation, is a position which shall be defended to the last drop of ink of,

A LOVER OF REASON AND GOOD SENSE,

YET, A STAUNCH BIBLIOMANIAC.

5. LETTER FROM J. K. TO MR. URBAN.

November 15, 1813.

MR. URBAN,—

I ADMIRE the ingenuity of your correspondent A. C., who appears to consider the preservation of "rare articles in Literature" as very praise-worthy. I cannot conceive how the preservation of books, merely because they are "old books," can be so very laudable. Nor can I give the collectors of these precious "rarities" full credit for an ardent thirst to contribute towards the advancement of Literature by such expensive means. If an old work be truly valuable, it will not be necessary to search monasteries, dive into vaults, pore over bookstalls, or grub up all the trash which has been consigned to the silence of centuries, and which, but for their officious zeal, would have been of much more service in the shops of cheesemongers, than on the gilded shelves to which they only operate as a foil. When have ever the really valuable productions of former ages, been suffered to lie

" High on a shelf neglected and forlorn ?"

Such works need not the industry of the Book-Collector, to rescue them from oblivion.   There are re-prints of them constantly issuing from the press for the instruction of mankind ; and thus are they preserved.   Yours, &c.

J. K.

6. LETTER TO BIBLIOMANIACKS IN GENERAL, AND TO THEIR LORD-SHIPS AND WORSHIPS, THE MEMBERS OF THE ROXBURGHE CLUB IN PARTICULAR.*

> " Pox on't," quoth Time to Thomas Hearne,
> " Whatever I forget, you learn ;"
> How blest the BIBLIOMANICS lot !
> *He learns what even Hearne forgot.*

MY LORDS AND GENTLEMEN,——
PERMIT me, without loss of time in ceremonious preface, to lay before your honours my pretensions, my services, and my misfortunes.   I am descended from a very antient family.   My ancestors of both sexes have, from the earliest ages of Literature, (even long before the invention of the art of printing) been renowned in every magnificent library for their attachment to books ; and numbers of our race have greatly distinguished themselves, so lately as within these last hundred years, by their assiduous and truly indefatigable labours in all kinds of works on the abstruser parts of general science, in ponderous *folios*, bulky *quartos*, and solid *octavos*, on Polemical Divinity, the Mathematicks, Algebraic computations, the Hebrew, and the higher order of Greek and Roman, of French, Italian, Spanish, German, and English Classicks.   Their critical acumen in numberless terms of grave controversial treatises has, at all times, been publicly acknowledged and attested ; although never adequately rewarded.   And yet it cannot be denied by their bitterest adversaries, that their silent toil—like the powerful " still small voice" of truth itself—has conduced more to *suppress* dull tracts, and to

* From the Gentleman's Magazine for December 1813.

compile new editions of good ones, than all the Edinburgh and Quarterly Reviews put together.

" Sed, genus, et proavos, et quæ non fecimus ipsi,"

my Lords and Gentlemen, I beg leave to assure you in the words of a Grecian warrior,—*translated into blank verse by Ovid, for the amusement of school-boys,*—" vix ea nostra voco."

I, too, am a critic! To *my* strong powers of argumentation, far more than to the reasonings of any Bishop on or off the Reverend Bench, is imputable the hopeless state of oblivion into which Priestley, Tom Paine, Horne Tooke, Brothers, Huntingdon, and Joanna Southcott, have fallen. I have fairly EATEN them *out of the field*, and *out of house and home* in any valuable Library. Such are among my services and pretensions. Let me now, alas! turn to my misfortunes.

How shall I begin? As a certain truly Trojan is by Virgil made beautifully to sing or say, " *Quis talia fando.*" . . . . ah! my tears! my tears! " *temperet a lacrymis?*" Cruel, barbarous " Bibliomania!"

Ever since the Rev. Thomas Frognall Dibdin's elegant publication under this all-imposing title has appeared, *like a comet*, blazing and illuminating the regions of occult studies, *my hopes are sunk, my occupations gone!* Had I a thousand mouths, arrayed with ten thousand double and single teeth, I could not regain the " spolia opima" that gentleman (with a head under his hat) has triumphantly taken from me and mine for ever!!!

A BOOK-WORM,

The British Museum   W. B**R.
  Attic Story.

7. MR. DIBDIN AND THE ROXBURGHE CLUB AT PARIS.*

IN the number of the Annales Encyclopédiques for July, Mr. Millin, Keeper of the Medals, &c. at the Royal Library, gives the following account

* From the Morning Chronicle of July 20, 1818.

of the celebration of the Roxburghe Anniversary at Paris by Mr. Dibdin, respecting which a short paragraph appeared in our Paper some days since :—

" While the members of the Roxburghe Club were celebrating, on the 17th of June, the memory of the first printers of the Boccacio at Venice, and in England, under the Presidentship of Lord Spencer, *the Honourable* Mr. Dibdin, *Vice-President*, united himself to this bibliographical banquet by a repetition of it, which he gave at Paris. He invited to it M. *Denon*, to whom France is yet indebted for a great portion of the Manuscripts, and early editions which she possesses, and several of the Conservators of the Royal Library, Messrs Vampraet, Langles, Gail, and Millin. It may be easily supposed, that Literary History and Bibliography offered an inexhaustible field for conversation ; the meeting displayed a mixture of gaiety and gravity becoming the banquets of the Muses ; and according to the ancient adage, the guests were more than three, and less than nine. M. Gail recited some Latin verses upon the occasion, the salt and spirit of which were not at first savoured by the guests, from the effect of the toasts. They will be printed in the Hermes Romanus.

Mr. Dibdin, the Amphitryon, and Chairman of the Meeting, proposed, as is customary, the first toasts :

1. The health of Lord Spencer, and the Honourable Members of the Roxburghe Club.

2. The memory of Christopher Valdarfer, printer of the Boccacio of 1471, the purchase of which, by the Duke of Marlborough, was the occasion of the formation of the Roxburghe Club.

3. The immortal memory of William Caxton, the first English printer.

4. The Glory of France.

5. The perpetual union of France and England.

6. The prosperity of the Royal Library of France :—and

7. The health of its worthy Conservators, whose knowledge is inexhaustible, and whose kindness is never weary.

8. The Propagation of Science, Art, and Literature, and of the Bibliomania.

9. May we meet again the same day in each year.

The guests returned these toasts by another, which was drank with hurrahs and three times three, according to the custom of England,—the health of the Vice-President of the Roxburghe Club, who did them the honour of assembling them.

The sitting terminated at the same hour the President quits the chair in London ; and the Vice-President, Mr. Dibdin, has carefully *preserved the corks*, to take to England, and exhibit as a memorial *of this* agreeable banquet." *

8. LETTER FROM VALDARFER, JUN. TO MR. URBAN.†

June 15, 1832.

MR. URBAN,—

IT has often been a matter of surprise and regret to the lovers of old literature, that, while our Northern neighbours of the Bannatyne Club have regularly transmitted copies to the British Museum, of *all* the curious works printed at their expense, the Roxburghers should not have followed this liberal example, not more than one third of these privately printed books, it is said being found in our great national repository. Each member, we believe, on his admission to the Roxburghe Club, undertakes to print, at his own cost, some curious and unique MS. or to reprint some very scarce and valuable book : a copy is delivered to every member, and a few more are struck off for presents. Surely the British Museum, though it cannot legally *claim* a copy, is eminently entitled to be enrolled in the list of donees. It were not well to turn onr backs upon the fountain of living waters, from which we have so often drawn the pure and limpid stream. But we need only scan the names of the noble Roxburghers, equally distinguished as patrons

---

* Dr. Dibdin says, in the *Second* Edition of his Tour in France, &c. that " these corks are yet (1829) in my possession : preserved in an old wooden box, with ribs of iron, of the time of Louis XI," vol. 2, p. 272.

† From the Gentleman's Magazine for July 1832.

of literature and the arts, and as scholars " ripe and good ones," to be convinced that in not transmitting *all* their valuable books to the Museum, they have been guilty of the sin of omission, rather than of *commission,* and that the slightest hint'will be sufficient to call their attention to the subject.

Hactenus hæc! As a sincere well-wisher to the Roxburghe Club, upon whose proceedings much obloquy has been cast by the " small wits " of the day, I cannot refuse myself the satisfaction of congratulating them upon the choice of editors to illustrate and explain the obsolete words and phrases found in these " Curiosities of Literature" which they have brought to light. And among the " nomina præclara et venerabilia," already registered in the Roll of Time, it were an injustice not to mention that of the acute and erudite Madden, whose commentaries upon " Havelock the Dane," and " William and the Werewolf," reflect the highest credit upon the author, and entitle him to the lasting gratitude of every lover of old English Literature.

Your's, &c.

VALDARFER, Jun.

For EU product safety concerns, contact us at Calle de José Abascal, 56–1°, 28003 Madrid, Spain or eugpsr@cambridge.org.